Presented to

From

Date

Endorsements

In my most recent book published by Charisma House, *The Passover Prophecies: How God is Realigning Hearts and Nations in Crisis*, I wrote, "We must be a people of imagination like the early pioneers of nations. Isaiah 26 is wonderfully translated in the Passion Translation Bible. I love the way verse 3 is phrased: *those whose imaginations are consumed with you* (Isa. 26:3). The Hebrew word translated "imagination" is *yester*, meaning "form, concept, framework, imagination, mind". A human imagination wholly owned by the Holy Spirit is one of the most powerful redemptive forces on earth.

These times call for a critical, God-filled imagination. This will create a new framework and conceptualization of all the problems around us. Our minds should be fixed on and become consumed by Him. This is what will unleash the supernatural creativity resident in all of the redeemed and will give birth to the exploits necessary for our triumph. In this season, we must reform our minds and imaginations. We must gather raw materials, then shape them into form and identify our future. Our concepts, frameworks, minds and imaginations must unlock into new forms and identities to meet and triumph in the era ahead.

Dr. Barbie Breathitt's five book series, *IMAGINE*, has captured the essence of God's plans to reinvent the church in the fullness of Christ's creative, life-giving, resurrection power with signs and wonders following. Each individual believer must take on his or her Christlike identity as a Son of God to move forward into this era, as One New Man arises to demonstrate God's glory on earth as it is in heaven!

Dr. Chuck D. Pierce
President, Glory of Zion International Ministries
President, Global Spheres in Corinth, Texas

God's ways are higher than our ways, and yet we are invited to co-labor with Christ as partakers in His divine nature. Pioneering ideas in her new book series *IMAGINE*, will open you up to your limitless potential. You will come to know that God created you to navigate life with the mind of Christ, and by faith, you can tap into a Spirit-inspired, creative process that is aligned with God's heart.

Dr. Breathitt's books will help you to understand your call to walk in a prophetic relationship with Jesus and to unlock the powerful truths available to all who believe in Him. This is a fresh invitation to imagine with God, to dream with Him for the future and to access and implement heaven's answers to the world's problems to advance God's Kingdom.

Dr. Ché Ahn
Founder and President, Harvest International Ministry
Founding and Senior Pastor, HROCK Church, Pasadena, CA
International Chancellor, Wagner University
Founder, Ché Ahn Ministries

Many copy or imitate others. Some create a model for others to learn from, and some are innovative. But few are innovators. Others learn a subject matter, then reach a peak and just plain plateau and cease advancing. Then there are those who become constant learners as a lifestyle, filling their heart and soul with the creative realms of God. Dr. Barbie Breathitt is cut from this type of creative fabric.

As an educator and prophetic interpreter/analyst, this consecrated woman of God consistently takes us on an exciting journey of discovery. Can you imagine that? As you partake of Barbie's teachings and her adventurous spirit carved from the boundaries of the Word of God, you, too, will grow in your prophetic imagination into a place where dreams really do come true!

Dr. James W Goll
Founder, God Encounters Ministries and GOLL Ideation LLC
Life Language Communications Coach

Dr. Barbie L. Breathitt is on the cutting edge of using her God-appointed seer gifting to help people gain an enhanced understanding of how God created and operates through the imagination, so that His people can apprehend the mysteries and purposes of God and manifest His glory in the earthly realm."

Cindy Jacobs
Generals International, Dallas, Texas

Beautiful, wonderful and full of divine insight! *IMAGINE* provides the 'missing link' in Christian understanding and practice between the natural and the supernatural realms that many believers have been seeking for years. Dr. Barbie Breathitt has done the body of Christ a great service by providing a solid biblical foundation for understanding how the natural and spiritual interact—how we integrate that process into our own lives by cooperating with the Holy Spirit.

These books are both paradigm changing and life altering. It is a wonderful blend of contemplative and analytical biblical thinking, personal experience building and divine revelation that will provide earnest believers with a new blueprint for the kind of walk with God they have always yearned for.

I suggest you read these books slowly and thoughtfully, perhaps several times, because it redefines the normative Christian experience in many fundamental ways. As you train your senses (Hebrews 5:14) this way, you will find yourself thinking all things have become new for me now.

Joan Hunter
Author/Healing Evangelist
Host, TV Show *Miracles Happen*

Dr. Barbie Breathitt's book series *IMAGINE* is a timely message, as this is the hour that God is releasing creative thinking and solutions from heaven. These books will open doorways to anointed thinking and the ability to see in the Spirit. This will activate your ability to dream and create at new levels through the Holy Spirit. This series is grounded in sound biblical teaching and practical instructions of how to apply it to your daily life. It is not just for creative dreamers, seers or songwriters—it is applicable to all the gifts, especially in business and ministry.

Doug Addison
Doug Addison.com
Author, webcast *Hearing God Everyday*, podcast *Daily Prophetic Words*, and prophetic blog *Spirit Connection*

Perfect, absolute peace surrounds those whose imaginations are consumed with you (Isaiah 26:3 TPT). Our imagination enables us to envision the Invisible One and thereby, as Barbie wrote, '...to redesign the image of ourselves.' The imagination is uncharted territory for Christians. We need more people like Dr. Breathitt to lead the way.

Ron Campbell

In her *IMAGINE* series, Dr. Barbie Breathitt's intensity of personae invites readers to partake in her deep insights, advanced levels of understanding and supernatural operations of faith in the glory realm. She challenges us not only to dream but also dares us to courageously imagine the impossible. Barbie creatively inspires us to unlock our potential in Christ through our imagination, to transcend the limitations of the flesh and progress in the limitless dimensions of God's glory.

I was often labeled as and teased about being a fantasizer during my childhood years, which greatly stifled the use of my imagination. The *IMAGINE* series has now unlocked the door to my imaginativeness, allowing me to freely and confidently advance. I have been awakened to the vast dimensions of God consciousness and His power, which equip me to exist and operate far beyond my God-given anointings and giftings. This series empowers me to live my future in the now!

Michael Adeyemi Adefarasin
Kingdom Lifeline Apostolic Ministries (KLAM), Abuja, Nigeria

A new era has dawned for God's people! A newfound season of supernatural revelation is being released from heaven to those who have the spiritual eyes and ears to see and hear what the Spirit is doing and saying (see Revelation 3:22).

Dr. Barbie Breathitt's *IMAGINE* series issues a clarion call for Believers to arise and supplant the old nature and attain their new identity in Christ. She implores readers to take on the very nature of Christ. She encourages them to utilize their divine imagination to create and decree their God-purposed destinies into reality in the same way God imagined and created before the beginning of time. Readers will discover the fundamental knowledge of how to apply their infinite imagination to shape their individual lives, influence the world and execute God's purposes.

Allow Barbie's *IMAGINE* series to transform your mind and usher you into a higher dimension of the Lord's destiny for your life!

Barbara Wentroble
President, International Breakthrough Ministries (IbM)
President, Breakthrough Business Leaders (BBL)
Author, Releasing the Voice of the Ekklesia; Becoming a Wealth Creator; Council Room of the Lord (series)

Works by the Author

Angels in God's Kingdom

Dream Encounters: Seeing Your Destiny from God's Perspective

Gateway to the Seer Realm: Look Again to See Beyond the Natural

So You Want to Change the World?

Hearing and Understanding the Voice of God

Dream Seer: Searching for the Face of the Invisible

Dream Interpreter

A to Z Dream Symbology Dictionary

Volume I Dream Symbols

Volume II Dream Symbols

Volume III Dream Symbols

Action Dream Symbols

When Will My Dreams Come True?

Dream Sexology

Sports & Recreation Dream Symbols

IMAGINE

RELEASING GOD'S CREATIVE POWER

Dr. Barbie Breathitt

VOLUME 4

IMAGINE: Releasing God's Creative Power

Breath of the Spirit Ministries, Inc.
P.O. Box 1356
Lake Dallas, Texas 75065
BarbieBreathitt.com
BarbieBreathittEnterprises.com
DreamsDecoder.com

ISBN-13: 978-1-942551-08-9

9 781942 551089

Published by: Barbie Breathitt Enterprises, Inc.

Printed in Canada.

Dedication

It is my deepest honor to dedicate my series of five *IMAGINE* books to my best friend, personal confidant and beautiful baby sister, Brenda Doreen Breathitt. She was born in Lakeland, Florida on October 29, 1966 and transitioned into Heaven on Saturday, September 7, 2019 at the age of fifty-two. Brenda was a brilliant light of joy with an excellent sense of humor that caused us all to laugh. Her warm, inviting smile disarmed people, letting them know she was a safe place to share their hearts. Brenda was clothed with grace, compassion and beauty that sprang up from a deep well within her loving heart. Her caring concern for others exuded from her countenance to bless all those who knew her. Brenda was full of godly strength and dignity.

Brenda's name meant *the glory of God's sword. Let all who seek You rejoice and be glad in You; and let those who love Your salvation say continually, let God be magnified* (Psalm 70:4). She laughed and loved well through her painful battle with cancer knowing in the days to come she had a home in heaven. Her thoughts and prayers were with her unsaved friends and family members that she was leaving behind. She spoke with wisdom and godly counsel always carrying faithful instruction on her tongue. She diligently watched over her family, friends and household never eating the bread of idleness. Her only daughter Chelsea arises to call her blessed. There are many women who do noble things, but Brenda's loving nature, quick wit, sterling character and integrity surpassed them all. We all know that charm is deceptive, and physical beauty is fleeting; but I praise Brenda for she was a woman who feared the Lord. Those who had the chance to know Brenda honor her memory for all that her hands have done. No matter where Brenda went she always found a friend. Her sweet words of comfort bring her praise from the city gates. Brenda blessed so many in her life with unconditional love, a listening ear, and words of encouragement, profound humor and a shared smile. Brenda made all of us better people for having known her. She is sorely missed.

Barbie

Thank You

A special thank you to heaven's Prophetic Poet Keat Wade for sharing the amazing poems he has authored in his four amazing books: *For Whom Beyond Beckons, Dueling Kingdoms: Chronicling the Times, A Gnarled Tree and Me,* and *Chronology of Love: Times and Seasons.* All of his incredible poems are available on Amazon.com and through Christian Publishing Xulon Press.

Keat Wade's poems are unique in three ways, (1) the supernatural way poems are received (2) the visual of what is going on in the supernatural realm (3) and being in sync with God's Timing (Hebrew Calendar). Keat Wade shares intimate conversations with the Almighty. He only writes what he hears. Keat hears or visually sees either the title or the first line. Nothing more comes until he starts to write. Then the words flow in poem form as a divine download, complete in one setting. Keat feels drawn into that supernatural realm until the words are complete. Then it lifts. The poems reflecting the Timing of God picture what God is doing in the supernatural realm, thus giving confirmation or direction.

Keat is a graduate of Fort Hays State University. He is a writer by desire and academically prepared with a Bachelor of Arts degree in English and Speech and a Master of Education degree in guidance and counseling. Keat retired from his teaching at Oklahoma Wesleyan University. Keat and Judy Garlow Wade now live in the San Diego area where his prophetic writing began.

Foreword

God is restoring our vision with provision.

Dr. Barbie Breathitt's *IMAGINE* series persuasively inspires Believers to embark on a journey of self-discovery, seeking and finding God and to discover His hidden, concealed mysteries through their sanctified imagination.

Readers will be immersed in God's truth and transformed by fresh revelation, soundly based on Scripture, crucial to this new season of operating in supernatural strength, powerful influence and Christ's authority. One is introduced to the aspects and mighty functions of the Holy Spirit, the Seven Spirits of God, God's communication conduits (dreams and visions) and how to use the awakened imagination to pray effectively, tap into unlimited favor and blessings, access healing and manifest miracles.

This is a new day of opportunity. Our divine imagination affords us the ability to know and receive all that God has destined for us to be and accomplish. It is time to increase and expand our borders. Barbie's writings challenge us to disconnect from the religious, legalistic ways of reasoning and exchange them for the creative, life-giving mind of Christ.

These volumes stir us to imagine the impossible, to consider how we think, what we believe and how we relate to God Almighty and others so that we can become Christlike, accurately discern God's plans and purposes and manifest His glory for His Kingdom advancement. Barbie has managed to successfully use applicable Scripture-based examples and captivating stories throughout the series to enlighten, encourage and guide us through a spiritual conversion of our identity that empowers us to apprehend our extraordinary future.

Our God-designed, ingenious imagination births visions of the unknown things of God and brings the invisible realms of creation into focus so it can become a reality in our lives. What we create and see in our imagination causes us to encounter and experience a broader dimension of God.

God's Spirit is advancing and positioning us through the use of our divine imagination to equip us with wisdom, revelation, fresh anointings and unlimited prosperity in order to draw the lost, sick and dying unto Christ.

Dr. John P. Kelly
Convener, International Coalition of Apostolic Leaders
InternationalCoalitionofApostolicLeaders.com

Contents

Introduction

This fourth volume of the *IMAGINE* series contains revelation regarding the healing power of the subconscious, God's imaginative power and creative miracles. As we come into agreement with God, we are able to release His creative power by using our sanctified imagination and prophetic voice. God desires for His people, as the Sons of God and as One New Man, to increase, prosper and advance for His kingdom purposes.

God is the Eternal One. There is no other living god besides Him. God is forever duplicating, expanding and giving expression to Himself in the multiple millions of individually unique souls of mankind. God has the power of life and death, to wound and to heal. No one can compare to Christ's creative power. We are created in God's image to carry the loving power of His presence!

We expand in our capacity to hold more of God by repenting of the sin that detracts, atrophies and weakens us. When we are forgiven and take on our Christlike character, we have the boldness to flex our godly strengths as our new and kingly identity is formed within us. As we spend time with Christ in the secret place of our imagination, God forms a new and Christlike uniqueness within each of us. Christ is waiting there at rest within us, resident in our imagination. Christ desires for us to discover the power of His presence so that we can display His glorious beauty. When mankind allows the creative power of God's love to override the sheer love of power, the world will finally know true peace.

We must first enter the door (consciousness of) Jesus. We cannot bring any part of our old, sinful, carnal nature or doubt-filled belief systems into our new conscious awareness that the fullness of God dwells within us. Jesus constantly left the earthly realm of natural manifestations to ascend into heaven during times of prayer in order to seek the face of His Father. Jesus left behind His consciousness of being a man, and He rose in God consciousness. Jesus became one with His Father in order to apprehend the wisdom and power needed to achieve the things that His Father desired for Him to do on earth. *Then He who sat on the throne said, "Behold, I make All Things fresh and new." And He said to me, "Write, for these words are true, dependable and faithful"* (Revelation 21:5).

To be transformed, we must first have a desire to be different and better. A true desire to change must arise from within our heart and our renewed, Christlike mind of our imagination, not from some twist of fate, chance or outer force. Our mind must be renewed in the Spirit of Christ in order to expect and experience positive changes in our life.

> *God desires for His people, as the Sons of God and as One New Man, to increase, prosper and advance for His kingdom purposes.*

To manifest our true self, we must imagine that we have already become that utmost person we desire to be. Our mental thoughts that meditate on the living Word of God and internal conversations of the tongue are responsible for creating the blueprints of our future. Blessed are the meek, those who have tamed their fiery tongue, for they shall inherit the earth. During the times we rest in God's presence (prayer) and prepare our heart (imagination) in peace, we are empowered to tread upon stinging scorpions and crush the venomous heads of snakes' lies under our heel.

The image of the *new you* must believe and feel that the transformation is real, permanent and sustainable in order for it to be actualized and maintained as fact. If the expected desire and your cultivating faith (we draw, by faith, the evidence of our godly convictions unto ourselves) are not mixed with the truth of God's Word, which empowers you to believe and act on your prophetic promises, you will continue to remain the same.

> *In the past people died in faith still believing but not receiving what God had promised them. They saw the manifestation of*

> *the promise from afar off distance, welcomed and embraced the promises, but they confessed they were strangers* (out of their comfort zone) *and pilgrims in a foreign land they did not know how to navigate* (Hebrews 11:13). *God having supplied something better for us* (Hebrews 11:40).

Today, nothing can separate us from the love of God. In All Things, we are more than conquerors through Christ Jesus who loves us (see Romans 8:37)!

We believe God with our heart and see the promises of God with our renewed mind in the realm of imagination. Even when they are afar off, we are assured of their existence. We receive them with intensity and repeatedly embrace and draw them to ourself with a determined dedication until we rest in and manifest all of our God-given promises. When we ponder and meditate on a particular promise that we have imagined, it will manifest.

We are told to continually study the Word of God, to meditate on it day and night, so we will be sure to remember and obey everything that is written therein. Only when the living Word of God is written on the tablets of our heart's 'imagination' will we prosper and succeed in all we do (see Joshua 1:8).

Likewise, it is necessary that you embrace a new and higher perception in order to successfully maintain your new, Christlike identity. Otherwise, the habitual actions of the carnal man will try to resurrect a mutiny to dethrone the new reigning king. Today, if we choose to listen to the commands of God and carefully obey them, the Lord will make us the head, not the tail. We will live above the status quo, always being on top, and we will never fall to the bottom again (see Deuteronomy 28:13).

> *As we mature spiritually, we must be disciplined in our thinking and in our actions.*

As we mature spiritually, we must be disciplined in our thinking, speech and actions. So many times, people say or pray one thing but end up being disappointed. For some reason or another, the prayer they prayed never receives a positive answer. One way we achieve disciplined thinking, speech and action is by developing and maintaining a servant's mindset and attitude, just like Jesus did. The disciplined, God-fearing imagination creates its world by faith.

Faith, prayer and the imagination are the creative forces that allow us to receive our God-imparted desires and achieve our God-purposed destiny. When coupled with consistent faith-filled prayer, the creative power of the imagination produces miraculous health, increase and success. The Bible tells us that we can pray for anything, and if we boldly believe that we have received (past tense verb) it, it will be ours (see Mark 11:24). On the contrary, doubt (the opposite of faith) and fear are weighty hindrances that cause our prayers to go unanswered, and they cause dis-ease, lack and poverty.

If we ever find ourselves astray, God is willing and faithful to forgive and restore us into right sonship. He waits and longs for His beloveds to return to Him, their first love, without bringing false condemnation or shame along with them. Imagine what the world would be like if everyone followed God's Golden Rule: Love One Another and do unto others as you would have them do unto you!

Because the Spirit of God is the creative force within our imagination, we have been given the spiritual power of imaginal sight.

The concepts we believe govern the outcome of our life. Our own self-concepts, personal assumptions, history and traditions (the private rulebook we follow) will determine who we are currently and, more importantly, who we are destined to become. Therefore, the things we believe as fact and the precepts that we hold fast to as truth form the ideas and construct the concepts by which we conduct our life. If any are false concepts, we will be riddled and paralyzed with fear. False concepts with which we agree are mental strongholds that must be renounced, repented of and torn down. Truth must take the place of any lie.

Our beliefs not only govern the outcome of our own life but also shape our world that surrounds us. In order to change our world, we must change our mind and repent of any sin or wrong, negative, corrupt inner speech or action. Because the Spirit of God is the creative force within our imagination, we have been given the spiritual power of imaginal sight. The Spirit of Christ abides in us to communicate His grand desires for us through our imagination. When we are born again of the Spirit and water, Christ gives our words the same power to produce life or death, to wound or to heal, to create, build up, diminish or tear down.

When our speech changes to match the internal voice of God, who is dwelling within us, the beliefs of our mind will also change to reflect God's truth and righteousness.

> *That you put off, concerning your former conduct, the old man which grows corrupt according to the deceitful lusts, and be renewed in the spirit of your mind, and that you put on the new man which was created according to God, in true righteousness and holiness* (Ephesians 4:22-24).

Our inner speech must agree with God's plans and mirror Holy Spirit's declarations. Then if we give prophetic voice to destiny, the transformation and the light of the new man dawns and emerges from the depths of our dark subconscious womb. It then explodes onto the surface, and it births the liberating light of God's revelation power. That which was once a private dream or an inaudible internal conversation held within our consciousness (when it is acted upon with faith) becomes an explosion of light that releases God's creative life force. For we all stumble in many things. *If anyone does not stumble in word, he is a perfect man, able also to bridle the whole body* (James 3:2).

CHAPTER ONE

New Kingdom Wineskins

The Bible makes it clear that we cannot put new wine in an old wineskin. This is because an old, dry wineskin is too small and not flexible. When the new, living wine continues to grow, it will expand and will crack and burst the tough, old wineskin. And, in kind, we never sew an old, thin, threadbare patch on a costly, new designer garment.

> *No one puts a piece of un-shrunk cloth on an old garment; for the patch pulls away from the garment, and the tear is made worse. Nor do they put new wine into old wineskins, or else the wineskins break, the wine is spilled, and the wineskins are ruined. But they put new wine into new wineskins, and both are preserved* (Matthew 9:16–17).

This is why Scripture warns us not to be like Lot's wife. She looked back with a desire to maintain or preserve her old, comfortable, worldly ways of life. She longed to return to the love of the world, where she had existed at a much lower level of being. Having turned from the new state of being and longing for the old ways of existence, Lot's wife died. She turned into a pillar of preserved salt. Remember Lot's wife. *Whoever seeks to save his life will lose it, and whoever loses his life to Me will preserve it* (Luke 17:32-33).

When Christ comes into us at salvation, we surrender everything to His powers, because All Things must become new. Throughout our Christian walk, we will determine that every new chapter of life is already complete and fully formed. The next expanding dimension or the subsequent realm (of the resulting spiritual mansion) is already complete in itself. To enter in, we must repent of sin, and we must change our outmoded ways of doing things, our archaic traditions that nullify God's power.

We must take on a new, Christlike image by becoming part of the One New Man. There is not any room for us to bring in our timeworn, outdated, critical and judgmental ways of thinking. We must leave behind our (former) poor, selfish attitudes, bad habits, lack of self-control or any other aspect of our old man's carnal nature. Having been renewed in Christ, we must only bring (new) acceptable, lovely and pure things into the storehouse. Thus, forsaking all others, we remain true to Jesus, our covenant lover.

Jesus obediently learned, mirrored and displayed on earth whatever He saw His Father doing in heaven.

Jesus Christ the Messiah is always the same yesterday, today and forever throughout all the ages (see Hebrews 13:7–8). Once Jesus discerned and knew the will of His Father in the heavenly mansions, He asked to gain an infusion of wisdom and power to accomplish His Father's will here on earth. Scripture states, *Christ is the Power of God and the Wisdom of God* (1 Corinthians 1:24). Jesus obediently learned, mirrored and displayed on earth whatever He saw His Father doing in heaven. Jesus declared in a solemn oath to us:

> *The Son is able to do nothing of Himself, of His own wisdom, power or accord; but He is only able to do what He sees His Father doing, for whatever the Father does in Heaven is what the Son mirrors and does in the same way on earth* (John 5:19).

Christ's diligence in seeking His Father gave Christ a 100 percent success rate. Jesus did nothing on His own. Jesus never functioned independently of His Father. Imagine what we could do if we followed Jesus Christ as our example (God's perfect prototype of the firstborn Son of many sons). Christ, the One New Man, did not do things by His own independent design or in His own strength or power. He was totally dependent upon seeing, mirroring and then doing what His Father did in a higher realm of existence.

> *For as the Father has life in Himself, so He has granted the Son to impart life in Himself, and has given Him authority to execute judgment also, because He is the Son of Man. Do not marvel at this; for the hour is coming in which all who are in the graves will hear His voice and come forth—those who have done good, will experience the resurrection into eternal life, and those who have done evil, will feel the resurrection of condemnation* (John 5:26–29).

When we, like Jesus, hear and answer the voice of the Holy Spirit calling to us, we are made alive, and we are completely transformed and renewed from the inside out. When the *new man* emerges, a fresh spiritual awareness of life's adventure begins. We cannot carry our old thoughts, identity, ways and habits into a new life if we want to maintain the health and presence of our new man. The old is gone; behold, All Things are new.

To maintain this new place of authority in Christ, we must continue to reject the lies found in our carnal nature, our false belief systems and others' erroneous opinions that are wrapped up in the traditions and superstitions of man. Like Isaac, we must become blind to the physical, objective outer world of Esau. Isaac blessed the smooth, soft, inner-spiritual Jacob who is supplanting our rough, external tendencies of hunting for things in this barren, desolate world. Now we execute judgment on the (previous) limited concepts of our old self-image.

> We have been given a new wineskin (a teachable heart) with the ability to perceive the secret and to imagine the hidden mysteries of God's Kingdom.

Through salvation, we embrace the never-changing truth of God. We receive eternal life, health, wealth and wisdom, and we harmonize in His peaceful presence. As born-again Believers, we resurrect from the grave as a new spiritual creature in Christ. We are full of Christ's divine-conscious nature that now so richly dwells within us.

> *Now see that I, even I AM He, and there is no God besides Me; I kill* (the old, sinful nature and bad habits) *and I make alive* (the new man in Christ*); I wound and I heal; nor is there any who can deliver from My hand* (Deuteronomy 32:39).

When we are born again, we are absent from our (former) dead body. Now we are reborn, living in a state that is present with the Lord. *We are confident, yes, well pleased rather to be absent from the body and to be present with the Lord* (2 Corinthians 5:8).

We are given the invitation to leave behind our old wineskin (concepts of our being) to become a new, flexible wineskin (new man creature) in Christ. Our physical body is the old man who must die to self in order to be born again, becoming the newly-created, flexible wineskin or expanding habitation for God. Leaving our present concept, we desire to become new and different. Otherwise, we will remain limited by the physical restrictions of our earthly body. We must become Christ-conscious instead of being self-conscious.

> To the believing, the imaginative realm of Christ holds the keys to liberate the Kingdom of God.

We cannot permanently change the reflection of our image just by stirring the water; for when the water stills, our reflection will revert back to being the same as it was before the new movement. The only way to change the way we appear, how we express ourselves or our countenance, is to change our consciousness, so that we imitate Christ. We reflect whatever and whomever we are conscious of believing or presently being.

> *For we know that if our body, the tent or earthly house, is destroyed or dissolved, we have an eternal spiritual body, a house or mansion, from God that is not made with hands in the heavens. While we are here on earth, we groan in our physical body, earnestly desiring to be clothed with our heavenly body as a garment and celestial habitation. So by putting on our heavenly spirit body, we shall not be found naked without a physical, earthly body. For while we are still in this earthly body or tent, we groan under the burden, being weighed down, oppressed and depressed, not that we want to put off the body, but we long to be further covered and clothed by the Spirit so that the mortal dying body may be swallowed up by eternal life after the resurrection. God fashioned us, preparing and making us fit for the Spirit's transformation, having given us the Holy Spirit as a guarantee.*

> *So then, we are full of God's goodness, hopefully confident and courageous; for we know that while we are at home in this physical body, we are away from our eternal mansion and absent from the Lord. For we walk by faith, regulating and conducting our lives by our convictions of divine things, trust in God, holy fervor and belief in Christ, not by sight, circumstances or the appearance of earthly things. To be absent from the body means to be eternally present with the Lord. Therefore, we should make it our desire and life-long goal, whether present or absent in the body, to be well pleasing to Him* (2 Corinthians 5:1–8).

By raising the level of our conscious focus on loving God, we also learn to hit the reset button to reappraise our own worth in Christ. When we realize that Christ so loved humanity that He gave Himself for us, we will reappraise and increase our own value. Being conscious that Jesus gave His all for us, we will, in turn, give our all to searching out, finding and loving the Christ within us.

> *IAM the Good Shepherd* (awareness) *who risks and lays down His own life for the sheep* (the different aspects of who IAM in Christ). *IAM knows and recognizes His own sheep. My sheep know My voice, recognize the appearance of My countenance and are conscious of My presence so, they follow Me. The Good Shepherd has never lost one sheep that His Father has given Him to steward* (John 10:11, 14).

> *The Lord is my Good Shepherd. He feeds, leads and guides me as my Provider and Shield of Protection so there is nothing that I lack. He makes me to lie down in fields of green pasture where the still waters run. He refreshes and restores my life so; I can rest and drink deep of His goodness. He escorts me in the paths of righteousness for IAM's name sake* (Psalm 23:1–3).

Since the Good Shepherd has given us everything that we admire (love, security, wealth, health, protection, wisdom and guidance), we should be conscious of concentrating on and applying these qualities and heavenly attributes instead of focusing on our daily need. *His sheep conduct themselves properly in an honorable righteous manner among the unbelievers. So, that although they may slander us as evildoers, they will also witness our good deeds and come to glorify God* (1 Peter 2:12).

Believers are able to hear the voice of God, see the moving of His Spirit and feel the tender touch of His mighty hand gently guiding them so that they can follow Christ's every move.

> *The divine mystery that has been hidden from ages and concealed from generations, but now this secret has been revealed, and unfolded to every saint to manifest. To Believers God willed to make known what are the heavenly riches of the glory of this mystery among the Gentile, which is Christ in you, the hope fulfilled of glory* (Colossians 1:26–27).

We have been given a new wineskin (a teachable heart) with the ability to perceive and imagine the secret and hidden mysteries of God's Kingdom.

But to those who do not have a listening heart, My words are merely stories. Even though they have eyes, they are blind to the true meaning of what I say, and even though they listen, they won't receive the full revelation (Luke 8:10).

Bring forth the blind people who have eyes and the deaf who have ears (Isaiah 43:8).

Hear now this, O foolish people without understanding or heart, who have eyes and see not, who have ears and hear not (Jeremiah 5:21).

But He said, "To you (the Believer) *it has been given to know the mysteries of the Kingdom of God, but to the rest* (the unbelieving) *it is given in parables, so that 'Seeing they may not see, and hearing they may not understand'"* (Luke 8:10).

Those with a stony heart do not understand God's Word. They think the parables are mere stories of people who never lived. They are blind to the deep spiritual meanings of the revelation knowledge God is sharing with Believers. Though they hear the sound of words being spoken, they do not hear with understanding. Their eyes are open with visual capability, yet they do not see, perceive or understand the spiritual images all around them.

To the believing, the imaginative realm of Christ holds the keys to liberate the Kingdom of God. The imagination empowers the creative forces that are only found in the unrestricted mind that is renewed and inspired by God's sustaining presence. The glory realm has its own spiritual language that must be communicated, understood and applied spirit to spirit. People who do not utilize their imaginations often have a difficult time connecting to a tripartite God (Father, Jesus Christ and Holy Spirit) who speaks, moves and communicates by His Spirit to the human spirit.

The imagination empowers the creative forces that are only found in the unrestricted mind that is renewed and inspired by God's sustaining presence.

Jesus emptied Himself of His divinity and came as a man so that I can take on His image and come into the power of Christ Jesus. Believers become Jesus' extended hands to save, heal and deliver others.

Examine yourselves as to whether you are in the faith. Test yourselves. Do you not know yourselves that Jesus Christ is living in you? Unless indeed you have not experienced His presence and are disqualified (2 Corinthians 13:5).

Simon Peter replied, "You are the Christ, the Son of the living God" (Matthew 16:16).

But Jesus kept silent. And the high priest said to Him, "I call upon you to swear by the living God, and tell us whether you are the Christ, the Son of God" (Matthew 26:63).

The Spirit of God speaks, touches, leads, guides and directs us from within the imagination of our being. We become the spiritual interpreters who explain dreams, visions and parables to the disciples of Jesus.

> *But you are not in the flesh but in the Spirit, if indeed the Spirit of God dwells in and empowers you. Now if anyone does not have the Spirit of Christ, he is not His and if Christ is in you, He lives His life through you! The body is dead because of sin, but the Spirit is life because of righteousness. But if the Spirit of Him who raised Jesus from the dead dwells in you, He who raised Christ from the dead will also give and breathe life into your mortal bodies through His life-giving Spirit who*

> *dwells in you* (Romans 8:9–11).

Since Christ lives within us, there is no way Christ can come any closer or be more of an intricate part of us than He already is. Our plea is to seek to know Him, learn how to discover His ways and walk in the light of His understanding.

> *But the righteousness of faith speaks in this way, "Do not say in your heart, 'Who will ascend into heaven* (that is, to bring Christ down from above)*?' or 'Who will descend into the abyss* (to bring Christ up from the dead)*?'" But what does it say? The Word is near you; it is in your mouth and in your heart* (the word of faith that we preach)*: that if you confess with your mouth the Lord Jesus and believe in your heart that God has raised Him from the dead, you will be saved. For with the heart one believes unto righteousness, and with the mouth confession is made unto salvation* (Romans 10:6–10).

Let Us Pray

Dear heavenly Father, we bow our hearts before You in prayer. We thank You that your life-giving Spirit dwells with us to empower us to live by the Spirit, not by the desires of the flesh. Give us a new heart of flesh that is tender and flexible like a new, supple wineskin. Lead and guide us in the ways of truth so that we are pleasing unto You. Give us spiritual perception so that we can seek out, apprehend and understand the mysteries of the Kingdom of God. We do not want to preserve the old ways of doing things. We want to perceive the new things that the Spirit of God is doing in this new era. Give us Your wisdom and understanding so that we can prosper in everything we do. Amen.

CHAPTER TWO

The Divine Imagination

Please take a moment to consider the following questions: When you think of God the Father, His Son, Jesus Christ, or the Holy Spirit, where do you see Him living and dwelling? Do you see Jesus living within you? Is Jesus seated on the throne of your heart? Or do you see Jesus seated on a throne in a heavenly place far away? Do you see Him as an exterior manifestation coming from outside your being? Or do you see Jesus as an internal power arising from within you?

Jesus said, "IAM with you always, even unto the end of the age." If this is true, how can Jesus return when He is already dwelling within, moving through and giving us our very life breath?

> *Then Jesus came close to them and said, "All the authority of the universe has been given to Me. Now go in My authority and make disciples of all nations, baptizing them in the name of the Father, the Son, and the Holy Spirit. And teach them to faithfully follow all that I have commanded you. And never forget that IAM with you every day, even to the completion of this age"* (Matthew 28:18–20).

God has the words of eternal life, so where else can we go to create anything? With God All Things are possible, even if it seems impossible to us (see Matthew 19:26). All Things are possible to all who believe in God (see Mark 9:23).

> *To you who believe in the name of the Son of God so that you will be assured and know without a doubt that you have eternal life. Since we have this confidence, we can also have great boldness before Him, for if we present any request agreeable to His will, He will hear us. And if we know that He hears us in whatever we ask, we also know that we have obtained the requests we ask of Him* (1 John 5:13–14).

The divine imagination has no restrictions. However, the human imagining has two conditions: we must believe that All Things are possible for whoever believes in God, and we must stop relying and making decisions based on the limitations of our physical senses. Our God is in the heavens. *But we know our God rules from the heavens and He takes delight in all that He does* (Psalm 115:3).

The divine imagination has no restrictions.

We also know that our God is omnipresent. *Whatever the Lord pleases He does, in heaven and in earth, in the seas and in all deep places* (Psalm 135:6).

Our God lives in heaven, on earth and in the deep places of the seas, and He also lives within the compassionate soul of the Believer.

Personal Reflection Moment

1. Do you not discern and understand that you are God's body, His temple, His sanctuary?
2. Do you believe that God's Spirit has His permanent dwelling in you individually and in others (corporately as the Church)?

We know from experience and recognize, believe and understand that God loves us. We are consciously aware that God cherishes us. God is love, so if we put our faith in Him, continually dwelling in His love, we will continue in God; for God continues to dwell within and adheres to us. The Bible confirms that the Kingdom of God is within the Believer.

> *Now when He was asked by the Pharisees when the Kingdom of God would come, He answered them and said, "The King-*

> *dom of God does not come with observation; nor will they say, 'See here!' or 'See there!' For, indeed, the Kingdom of God is within you* (Luke 17:20–21).

Therefore, we know that there is an internal heaven and an external heaven, from which God rules, which can be manifested in and through the Believer.

The undisciplined imagination does as it pleases. The idols they create are made by human hands of silver and gold. They have mouths but speak not, eyes that do not see, ears that do not hear, noses that do not smell. They have hands but do not handle, feet but do not walk. Those who make them are like them; so is everyone who believes and trusts in them (see Psalm 115:4–8).

The disciplined, God-fearing imagination creates its world by faith. Faith, prayer and the imagination are the creative forces that require time to manifest.

> *I will stand at my guard post and station myself on the tower. I will keep watch to see what He will say to me, and what answer I will give as His prophetic spokesman when IAM approved. Then the Lord answered me and said, "Write My answer to the vision and engrave it plainly on tablets of clay* (people's hearts) *so that the one who reads it will run to carry the correct message to others. This vision is for an appointed time in the future. It hurries towards the goal, it describes the end and it will be fulfilled, it will not fail. If it seems delayed or slow in coming, wait patiently, for it will surely take place. It will not be overdue"* (Habakkuk 2:1–3).

God and His creative force exist within us, and we have our being in Him. Since God is living within me and moving through my imagination, I can believe my imagination! Jesus preached that the kingdom of heaven was at hand. Jesus taught that those who did the will of His Father would enter into the kingdom of heaven. He also preached a baptism of repentance, stating that for man to

The disciplined, God-fearing imagination creates its world by faith.

enter into the kingdom of heaven, he must humble himself, be converted and become like an innocent, imaginative child. Jesus told His disciples that (for these few reasons) it is very difficult for a rich person, who trusts in his wealth and own abilities, to enter the kingdom of heaven.

What is faith? Faith is the subjective appropriation of the hope we have for a prosperous future. To manifest a desire from the primal state of what is or was wished, simply create a scene that is true. Then concentrate on staying focused on seeing, feeling and hearing the result until that thing has come into being.

In Psalm 42, instructions on how to use the imagination to achieve desires are given to the pure and shining ones:

> *I long to drink of You, O God, drinking deeply from the streams of pleasure flowing from Your presence. My longings overwhelm me for more of You! My soul thirsts, pants, and longs for the living God. I want to come and see the face of God. Day and night my tears keep falling and my heart keeps crying for Your help while my enemies mock me over and over, saying, "Where is this God of yours? Why doesn't He help you?"*
>
> *So, I speak over my heartbroken soul, "Take courage. Remember when you used to be right out front leading the procession of praise when the great crowd of worshipers gathered to go into the presence of the Lord? You shouted with joy as the sound of passionate celebration filled the air and the joyous multitude of lovers honored the festival of the Lord! So then, my soul, why would you be depressed? Why would you sink into despair? Just keep hoping and waiting on God, your Savior." For no matter what, I will still sing with praise, for living before His face is my saving grace!*
>
> *Here I am depressed and downcast. Yet I will still remember You as I ponder the place where Your glory streams down from the mighty mountaintops, lofty and majestic—the mountains of Your awesome presence. My deep need calls out to the deep kindness of Your love. Your waterfall of weeping sent waves of sorrow over my soul, carrying me away, cascading over me like*

a thundering cascading torrent.

Yet all day long God's promises of love pour over me. Through the night I sing His songs, for my prayer to God has become my life. I will say to God, "You are my mountain of strength; how could you forget me? Why must I suffer this vile oppression of my enemies—these heartless tormentors who are out to kill me?" Their wounding words pierce my heart over and over while they say, "Where is this God of yours?"

So, I say to my soul, "Don't be discouraged. Don't be disturbed. For I know my God will break through for me." Then I'll have plenty of reasons to praise Him all over again. Yes, living before His face is my saving grace!

Jesus Christ our Redeemer is not of this world; He is from above. We are encouraged to lift our eyes up to be elevated into the realm of the Spirit, to relate to God in truth with a spirit to spirit interchange. Jesus is the only begotten Son of our heavenly Father. We experience the realization of His presence when we are born again from above by the Spirit and water. Salvation opens our spiritual eyes to see that Jesus is the only door (conscious reality) of entrance into the kingdom of heaven. *And I have also given you what you have not asked: both riches and honor, so that there shall not be anyone like you among the kings all your days* (1Kings 3:13).

> *Fear violently opposes faith, and it stops us from reaching our full potential.*

Let Us Pray

Dear Lord Jesus, let us have a vision of You living big and bold within us, not residing in some far-off heavenly place. We ask that You sit upon the throne of our heart. For Your Word says that You are with us always, even unto the end of the age. Teach us how to exercise Your authority and how to make disciples all over the earth. We know that nothing is too difficult for You. Thank you that Your divine imagination working within us has no restrictions. We place our trust and total belief in You, our Lord and Savior. Thank you for making Your abiding Kingdom within us, Your Believers. Help us to place our full measure of faith in You so that we can obtain a prosperous future. Open our spiritual eyes to see that Christ Jesus is the only door to eternal life. Amen.

CHAPTER THREE

Fresh Vision

When we enter into Christ at salvation and the Holy Spirit enters into us, we are immersed by the Spirit so that we can become one with God. We are given the overlapping, intermingled spiritual power of imaginal sight. The Lord is my eternal shepherd; I shall not want, for He always cares for me (see Psalm 23:1). Once we see the goodness of God living inside of us, even when we are surrounded by enemies and death calls for our soul in the midst of the battle, we remain steadfast, confident and unmoved (see Psalm 27:3).

We are so bold that we gladly cut ties with all restrictions of gender, race, creed, age and especially the restrictive religious traditions of our ancestors (see Galatians 1:14) to become the One New Man in Christ. *For all the land which you see I give to you and your descendants to possess forever* (Genesis 13:15). Habitual rituals nullify the ability of the creative power of God working in our life, but when we seek the Kingdom of God and His righteousness first, we are thrust into the deeper realms of the Spirit.

It pleases God to forgive our sins. He calls us before we are born, and by His kindness, He chooses to separate us unto Himself as the Sons of God. It is by God's great grace that He revealed His only begotten Son, Jesus, in and to us, so we can declare His glory to the nations (see Galatians 1:15–16). *For we did not choose Christ, He chose us* (John 15:6).

When we awaken to the fact that the Spirit of Christ abides in us to communicate His grand desires for us through our imagination, we learn to expect to live a supernatural, miracle-filled life. God's still, small voice instructs and eagerly bids us to accomplish amazing feats and to do great and mighty things. But before Christ was revealed to us, we did not know the expanse of the calling to greatness—to become even greater in Christ—that rests upon each of us. Believers in Christ become extraordinary beings that are no longer just ordinary people. Because of Christ living largely in us, we are powerful people who are supernaturally healthy, wealthy and wise. The spirit and soul that live within your body is your true, eternal self.

When Christ is being mirrored in us as our own conscious awareness of God, He becomes the fact of the high standard by which we measure what we can apprehend as our own end result.

In the glory realm, the Spirit's light frequencies of resonating sounds and the colors of the soul are as tangible and visible as our physical body of flesh is in the natural world. For our spirit man to grow, we must study to learn how to nurture, feed and develop our spirit man's strength in faith through the spiritual wisdom and communion with a holy God.

> *For though by this time you ought to be teachers, you need someone to teach you again the first principles of the oracles of God; and you have come to need milk and not solid food. For everyone who partakes only of milk is unskilled in the word of righteousness, for he is a babe. But solid food belongs to those who are of full age, that is, those who by reason of use have their senses exercised to discern both good and evil* (Hebrews 5:12–14).

By embracing God's desire as our own inner longing, we can envision the reflection of Christ. When Christ is being mirrored in us as our own conscious awareness of God, He becomes the fact of the high standard by which we measure what we can apprehend as our own end result. When we focus on Christ as our example, our thought processes rise. The mind of Christ transforms our current belief systems, advancing them into a higher spiritual dimension. We can see as a now reality what our new self looks like when it is manifesting the end result of who we are in Christ.

The imprinting of an actualized vision in our spirit is always more powerful than just thinking of a variety of possibilities or options that may or may not come into being. *Therefore you shall lay up these words of mine in your heart and in your soul, and bind them as a sign on your hand, and they shall be as frontlets between your eyes* (Deuteronomy 11:18).

If the thoughts and intents of our heart match those of the mind of Christ, this spiritual power of agreement of touching anything on earth causes the desire of our heart to be seen and boldly decreed. It is then able to be manifested and established by God. Our physical actions are birthed from the womb of our inner thoughts and our heartfelt desires and beliefs. *And the Lord your God will circumcise your heart and the heart of your descendants, to love the Lord your God with all your heart and with all your soul, that you may live* (Deuteronomy 30:6).

Forgiveness

We remain the same until we learn to forgive our present and past in order to gain the clarity of vision for the future. When we are bound by sin, we can only see what kind of person we were in the past or present. Forgiveness sets us free from our old nature. It's like being healed from our infirmity, taking up our bed of affliction and learning to walk again.

Forgiveness allows you to see the formation of the new you. It allows you to be transformed into the grand person of destiny that God has planned for you to be. If you forgive, you will be forgiven.

Tragically, if we do not forgive and release others from our bitter judgment (bless and not curse them) and then move on to a new, healthy chapter in life, we become fixated on a traumatic or negative event. By placing our focused attention on the person or persons who have offended, abused, hurt or rejected us, we empower them to control, change and transform us into their hostile image and destructive likeness. Constantly dwelling and focusing upon those persons and their actions

We remain the same until we learn to forgive our present and past in order to gain the clarity of vision for the future.

toward us activates our imagination to think like they think. Therefore, we subconsciously take on their abusive attributes and actions, repeating the vicious, detrimental cycle that we experienced. We end up harming those around us, becoming just like the persons we abhor.

Work at getting along with each other and with God. Watch over each other to make sure that no one misses the revelation of God's grace and favor. Keep a sharp eye out for weeds of bitter discontent. Otherwise, you'll never get so much as a glimpse of God. Make sure no one gets left out of God's generosity. And make sure no one lives with a root of bitterness sprouting within them, which will only cause trouble. This will throw people off the right path, and it will poison the hearts of many. A thistle (or a thorn bush) or two gone to seed can ruin the beauty of the whole garden in no time. Watch out for the Esau syndrome: trading away God's lifelong covenant gift in order to satisfy a short-term fleshly appetite. *You well know how Esau later regretted that impulsive act, sought and wanted God's blessing—but by then it was too late, tears or no tears* (Hebrews 12:15–17).

Forgiveness creates a new life vision that buries the old man with his former, and quite limited, states of mind.

True forgiveness comes from a heartfelt desire to change. We should forgive because we sincerely want to forgive a person, not out of obligation. *Forgive and you shall be forgiven* (Luke 6:37). Forgiveness creates a new life vision that buries the old man with his former and quite limited states of mind. Forgiveness has the power to revise, heal and resurrect a totally different and liberated person. *And a man's enemies will be those of his own household* (Matthew 10:36).

We are the temple of God; our body is the house of God. The sinful things we do and the wrong beliefs that are contrary to God are our personal enemies. Forgiveness is a pleasant path that leads to inner peace, a conquest over every opponent (see Proverbs 3:17). But when we forgive out of a sense of duty, not with a heartfelt desire to see another achieve their utmost and highest, our motivation is selfish, and it comes from a judgmental, legalistic source of pride.

We see, listen and relate to people according to the opinions we have formed about them. If we want someone to change, it is us who must first change our opinion of him or her. After all, he or she is only reflecting the false image that we have projected. We must stop being judgmental and critical of others. Sever all ties that tether you to the earthly, carnal realm.

> *But that you may know that the Son of Man has power on earth to forgive sins—then He said to the paralytic, "Arise, take up your bed, and go to your house." And he arose and departed to his house. Now when the multitudes saw it, they marveled and glorified God, who had given such power to men* (Matthew 9:6–8).

If someone criticizes us for a false belief, wrong concept or poor character trait, we should rejoice instead of being insulted, getting mad or carrying a grudge against that person. Now that we are aware of a sin or moral weakness, we have an opportunity to repent and remove that flaw or weakness to develop a stronger, more excellent character.

Criticism cannot harm us when we have learned to master our emotions, thoughts and reactions in a positive manner. Those who sought to criticize or hurt us have actually been used to enhance, advance and increase us. Now we have an opportunity to change for the better by improving ourself. Instead of thinking ill, hostile or resentful thoughts toward our accusers, reaping the myriad of maladies that these poisonous thoughts would produce, we can choose to prayerfully bless them in return. Positive, faith-filled prayer enriches, adjusts and enhances our actions. But prayer on behalf of the critical person also alters the way that that judgmental person will see and react to us in the future. Therefore, both prayer for ourselves and prayer for our accusers profit us.

Criticism cannot harm us when we have learned to master our emotions, thoughts and reactions in a positive manner.

Quickly forgive yourself for any wrong doing or flaws. Determine to make the necessary changes to do things differently. Then forgive and bless the accusers. Learn to recognize lies. Capture and cast down any vain, inflammatory imaginations or adverse thought patterns that may try to arise. Release God's love, and rejoice over an opportunity to sow goodwill. Get stronger, and grow into a better person through positively amending a difficult situation. God's grace will propel you onto a higher plane of peace.

When we are at harmony with God, we are empowered to bless those who have cursed and despitefully used us. A godly blessing is always more powerful than an evil curse. *Bless those who persecute you who are cruel in their attitude toward you; bless and do not curse them* (Romans 12:4). When we bless someone, it affords them the opportunity to rise above their previous or current circumstances, providing them the ability to advance, succeed and prosper in a new and different way.

Time for Change

We must stop lying in the bed of affliction. The battles we engage come from the internal thoughts and core beliefs that we entertain. There are two dominate thoughts. One is of the kingdom of light and the other is of the kingdom of darkness. The inner thoughts of our imagination form our outer actions, determining in which kingdom we reside. If we do not conquer a negative thought life, it will take up residence and build a mental stronghold in our mind. But if we tear down this fabricated fortress of lies brick by brick, and if we replace the adverse, deceptive, harmful thoughts with the positive building stones of life-giving thoughts, our imagination will produce a beautiful, godly and optimistic world vision.

Dreams and visions appear at the crossroads of life to confront us with the cross of Jesus. Will we hold onto the promises of God, believe His Word and risk entering into another process of transformation? Change is always necessary to ascend into the realm of faith. If we refuse the opportunity to change, we choose to remain the same ordinary, limited person, locked up and bound in the earthly realm.

> *We must stop lying in the bed of affliction. The battles we engage come from the internal thoughts and beliefs that we entertain.*

Change has a level of risk because we are letting go of both our past and the familiar comforts of the present. Imaginative dreaming enables us to increase our measure of faith as we move forward to possess and broaden our future opportunities. Great faith is necessary to acquire the knowledge and wisdom we need in order to be successful.

By seeing, believing for and agreeing with our previously unknown future, we can prayerfully determine which is the highest and best future to decree, and we can bring it into our now. Our past does not dictate the boundaries of our future. Our history lets us know where our fallow areas are that need to be broken up to repair breaches and mistakes in order to rebuild a bigger platform. Our past is only a fading memory that cannot keep us from entering into the power of who we are intended to be in the future unless we consciously continue to reside there.

The Holy Spirit empowers us to overcome the past. He encourages us to release the present. He teaches us how to stretch, reach for, grasp, take hold of and pull the best future into our now. God has placed a small piece of eternity in the hearts of all men to draw them unto Himself. God has made everything beautiful in its time. *Also, He has put eternity in their hearts, except that no one can find out the vastness of the work that God does from beginning to end* (Ecclesiastes 3:11).

As spirit beings, we constantly struggle with being connected to the pull of two very different realms at the same time. *And Jesus said to them, "You are from beneath; I am from above. You are of this world; I am not of this world"* (John 8:23). Jesus is the transitional bridge that links us or reconnects our transformational processes on earth to heaven's higher call.

When our mind is renewed by the living Word of God, we can embrace God's perfect will.

Most people dwell in the vertical earthly realm of double-minded confusion. This is where evil dominates through self-seeking motives. Sin operates in and through a sensual spirit, a demonic entity or by human wisdom. However, there are remnants of Believers who have transformed their mind by believing, reading, meditating on, receiving, applying and obeying the Word of God.

When our mind is renewed by the living Word of God, we can embrace God's perfect will. The Word of God equips us to live in the power of God's pure truth; for to the pure, All Things are pure. It is useless to try to change people. We are to focus on sanctifying ourselves, not on judging others. We are called to be saints sanctified by God the Father and preserved in Jesus Christ. People are only the witnesses who observe, listen to and tell us what they see in us. If we change our self-concept to become our ideal self, people will have to change their report of us as well.

The Bible teaches that we are not to be conformed to this natural world. We are to be transformed by the renewing of our mind so that we may prove (be transformed into the image of God) what is good, acceptable and the perfect will of God (see Romans 12:2). God's truth is eternal; therefore, He relates to us from the eternal, future-present Spirit of Truth.

The Holy Spirit leads and guides us upward through the transitional stages that empower us to enter into the future and bring it into our now.

The Holy Spirit leads and guides us upward through the transitional stages that empower us to enter into the future and bring it into our now. We ascend into the heavenly realms to obtain the truth of who we are currently. But more importantly, from this heavenly perspective, we gain a meek wisdom and godly understanding from the spiritual vision we see of who we will become in the future.

To experience a lasting change in our nature, we must consciously rise to a new level of godly desire. Now as we learn to act differently, we can continue to dwell in this higher state. We maintain that image until we are able to give a fresh expression of what we have seen and done. We do this until our new state of existence feels natural for us to be and remain there. This is how we become what we have seen.

At every one of life's crossroads, we must learn to activate our imagination to see a new, higher and formational vision for our future. If we do not learn to look ahead to see the hope of God's high calling moving us into something different, we will lack revelation knowledge. We will stagnate and perish. The Bible states that without fresh vision, people perish.

Let Us Pray

Thank you, Lord, that You are my loving shepherd. For I know that deep within You is everything that I need, want and desire. Help me to see myself living in an unlimited manner, not relating to people through my gender, race, creed, age or earthly identity. I need to look past any perceived limitations in order to break out of anything that would restrain me.

What concept in your life continues to limit you from becoming all you are called to be in Christ?

Lord, point out my weaknesses so I can repent, and help me see how they limit me from prospering. Help me to trust You as I emerge in my new, unlimited identity. IAM not just a male or female. IAM not limited to a specific race or age. IAM a divine Believer who is in love with Jesus Christ. IAM able to take off all limitations of the old wineskin. IAM able to step into a new, flexible wineskin. IAM growing, maturing, increasing and multiplying in every good way. Nothing is too difficult for me as I take on the identity and authority of Christ Jesus. Amen.

CHAPTER FOUR

The Healing Power of the Subconscious

As Believers, we know that Christ resides within us; therefore, the healing power of Christ is also within us. We've learned about man's natures and the workings of the subconscious previously. If you would like a more detailed refresher, please refer directly to Man's Minds and Dueling Natures and The Imagination chapters in Volume I.

The sinful attitudes of the carnal man always battle with the enlightened, spiritual man for control. These contrary natures constantly war with each other for dominion. The conscious mind is the reasoning, logical part of the mind. This is where we make our choices and decisions and develop our personal belief systems.

The subconscious mind perceives through our spiritual intuition without using any of our natural senses. It uses our spiritual gifts to gather revelatory insights. Our spiritual senses are able to see, hear, taste, feel or smell at a much higher level than our five natural senses. Believers must learn to see with their higher spiritual senses the imperceptible, to discern the indiscernible and to detect, know and respond to the obscure, concealed mysteries in the invisible realm. The subconscious mind is always receptive to the thoughts and plans of the conscious mind.

Our prayerful words and reverential actions open spiritual doors of consciousness. Once entered, these various access points place us in touch with God's higher truths from which we can form our concepts of truth and explore our spiritual perceptions. *Not by might, nor by power, but by My Spirit, says the Lord Almighty—you will succeed because of My Spirit, though you are few and weak* (Zechariah 4:6).

The power of God's life-giving Spirit is the internal force that frees us from the vicious loop of sin and death. Obedience to the Holy Spirit leads to life and peace, while following after our old ways leads to sin and death. The Spirit of the Lord gives life and freedom from trying to be saved by keeping a list of religious dos and don'ts. When the spirit of the Word of God is securely planted within our subconscious being, we can know the unseen, for the Word of God is Spirit and Life. Job said it this way: *For the Spirit of God has made me, and the breath of the Almighty gives me life* (Job 33:4).

The sinful attitudes of the carnal man always battle with the enlightened, spiritual man for control.

The spiritually attuned Believer can discern a person's inner reflections, beliefs, inspirations, judgements and contemplations. The Word of God within us will reveal another's focused resolves, hidden goals and concealed objectives. God's Word will also expose the disguised plans of others' heart purposes that they have veiled toward us or others.

> *For the Word of God is living and powerful, and sharper than any two-edged sword, piercing even to the division of soul and spirit, and of joints and marrow, and is a discerner of the thoughts and intents of the heart* (Hebrews 4:12).

Believers live within the shadow of the Almighty's refuge, sheltered from the time of trouble by the God who is above all gods.

Declare: He alone is my place of safety; He is my God who fills heaven and earth, and IAM trusting Him. He rescues me from every trap and protects me from the fatal plague. God hides me in His pavilion; in the secret place of His presence. He sets me in the cleft of the high rock, Jesus, where I see His lovely face and hear His sweet voice declaring things that are right and true. He keeps me safe from the plots of evil men and from the strife generated by their tongues. When I call, His thunder delivers me.

As we persist in walking in God's realm of favor, the prophetic words we have received, prayers that we have prayed, the hopes of what we desire to achieve and the dreams that we aspire to obtain in the future suddenly appear as facts that cannot be denied. Because we don't focus our attention on what is seen, but on what is unseen. *For what is seen is temporary, but the unseen realm is eternal* (2 Corinthians 4:18).

The power of the Holy Spirit transforms us through the still, small voice, the creative, life-giving dreams or visions and the rhema Word of God. We come to know more of God through the discerning of spirits, angelic visitations and the slight impulses or impressions in our subconscious inner knower.

The subconscious responds to our beliefs, inner voice and emotional feelings, and it is dedicated to reproducing what we habitually think upon. The subconscious is faithful to persevere in its course of action to carry out our beliefs, even in the face of difficulty or with little prospects of success. Therefore, it is important to constantly think good, wholesome thoughts about those we are relating to in life. If we think on positive, life-giving and creative thoughts, we draw those beautiful images and people into our life.

> *Believers must learn to see with their higher spiritual senses the imperceptible, to discern the indiscernible and to detect, know and respond to the obscure, concealed mysteries in the invisible realm.*

The subconscious is always recording our inner thoughts, motivations, stimuli and feelings. It is our reactive moods and sensations that bind us to a particular spiritual sphere. The subconscious helps to determine the divine mansion where we currently reside. The subconscious affects the way we act in our family and the way we relate to tribal people or different races. It determines how we enjoy our present career, and it impacts our belief system. The subconscious also determines the health of our emotional state of being, and it can even prompt or control the national geography we occupy.

God's perfect love casts out all fear when we realize that we are totally accepted in the Beloved. An emotionally mature person is gentle, kind, long-suffering, loving and understanding. He or she patiently embraces diversity and forgives others in order to live in harmony. The wise person will profit by learning from others, even those who hold a different point of view.

When the subconscious is positively united with the power of consistent prayer, its creative force produces health, wealth, increase, promotion, success and a blessed life of righteousness that is full of miracles. *He shall pray to God, and He will delight in him, He shall see His face with joy, for He restores to man His righteousness* (Job 33:26). Throughout our entire life, the subconscious will record all of our memories. These interesting happenings, diverse people, amazing objects, events and life desires are used to produce our dreams.

> Our prayerful words and reverential actions open spiritual doors of consciousness.

Our dreams reveal our highest calling and plans and the answers we seek. At every one of life's crossroads, it is necessary to pray, trust and believe that our subconscious thoughts will use godly wisdom to direct or redirect us at every level to the most maximized possible path. It is the subconscious that searches the heart. The subconscious gains the necessary spiritual understanding so that it can release the answer to life's toughest questions. To succeed, we need to learn how to follow our inner awareness of wisdom when there is a feeling of peace and prosperity.

The subconscious mind, like God, never sleeps or slumbers in its quest for foreknowledge. The subconscious is always reaching out, searching for spiritual gateways, so that it can travel spiritual paths in its unending search for God. The subconscious tries to discover healing answers in the invisible realm of divine wisdom. If we have ever gone somewhere, even once, in a vertical spiritual plain, our soul maps out the steps to the trip. Then our spirit memorizes the path of our journey so that we can quickly go there, returning again and again.

God is visiting our subconscious womb. The angelic realm visits us with a clear message from God. The Holy Spirit is overshadowing us with vision (His profound ideas) to impregnate us, just as He did with Jesus' mother,

Mary. The name Mary represents flowing water that runs into and fills the shape of empty spaces. The washing of the water of the Word that came through the angel cleansed and renewed Mary. The Holy Spirit overshadowed and impregnated Mary without the touch, help or knowledge of any man.

When the Holy Spirit comes to increase our imagination, we feel His presence moving in us so that we can birth a more creative, powerful and insightful destiny. When the subconscious feels and imagines something, the subconscious entertains that sensation until it is seen, felt and then becomes a present fact. Our continued and trained focus gives our feelings life until they manifest as facts with an active expression.

Our personal feelings, emotions and physical or spiritual sensations we experience are foundational for our realization of something desired. Because impressions always come before we take action, our feelings, moods and senses motivate us. The impressions we feel determine the response and attitude we display. Our belief will govern the strength of the manifestation of power that will follow us. Miraculous signs follow those who believe in the healing power of Christ within. Signs and wonders never precede our ability to birth positive feelings, images and ideas on a higher level of sustainable, focused faith.

> *The subconscious is faithful to persevere in its course of action to carry out our beliefs, even in the face of difficulty or little prospects of success.*

Never give a place for any negative emotion to take root. Do not allow even one disparaging impression to take up residence within your mind. Always capture, remove and cast down undesirable, adverse or harmful thoughts. Be sure to eliminate any depressed moods. Replace all detractors with the more powerful, life-giving force of God.

The presence of God transcends all barriers. He gives us an optimistic feeling of well-being and confidence. God showers us with His bold, progressive ideas. If our emotions are continually suppressed by destructive thoughts, outside accusations, constant criticism and judgmental assaults that cause feelings of failure, shame, depression or regret, our body reacts to the lack of joy and harmonious peace by developing a state of dis-ease.

When we repent of sin, doing evil or thinking in a wrong manner, the mind is renewed with the washing of the living Word of God and the Holy Spirit. We can change the way we think, believe, react and how our body responds. When our thoughts change, so do the actions of our body. *The manner in which we wish to be treated by others is how we should treat everyone else* (Luke 6:31). When we change the thoughts of our subconscious, we create change in our inner and outer world around us. By positively or negatively altering our actions, we change our future by exchanging it for either a higher destiny or a lower purpose.

> *When the Holy Spirit comes to increase our imagination, we feel His presence moving in us so that we can birth a more creative, powerful and insightful destiny.*

The ways of the Spirit are very intentional. Nothing happens by chance. The subconscious responds to the feelings that we portray as truth to it. If we feel something is true (to us, it is true), our subconscious will record it as a fact—a personal, undeniable truth. This is how the miracle-working power of God manifests healing in the body of a person suffering from a terminal disease.

If a person receiving prayer believes the Word of God is true, his or her subconscious receives the idea as truth. Then the subconscious creates a positive image of health and wholeness. Now the power and light contained in the living Word of Truth is injected. The light of God is released to expand within his or her body, pushing out all darkness and rejecting disease, until the anointing breaks the yoke to heal them.

> *Then My favor will bathe you in sunlight until you are like the dawn bursting through a dark night. And then suddenly your healing will manifest. You will see your righteousness march out before you, and the glory of Yahweh will protect you from all harm* (Isaiah 58:8)*!*

The subconscious never argues with what the conscious is showing or telling it. The subconscious does not alter or amend the truth; it only accepts and internalizes it. The subconscious will portray what it is told. *The centurion said, "Master, only speak the Word and my servant boy will be healed"* (Matthew 8:8). The subconscious always mirrors what it is shown. It announces details in the exact same manner in which they were received.

The subconscious will project images of a healthy body (for example, the wholeness of a new organ) into the imagination of that person. When the person sees and believes that he or she has been healed, the body responds to the subconscious' suggestion as a reality of truth. *Let us hold fast the confession of our hope without wavering, for He who promised is faithful* (Hebrews 10:23). The Spirit of Truth enters into someone's reality to set that person free by liberating him or her from a diseased state.

In the realms of the subconscious imagination, there is nothing that is impossible when man comes into agreement with the healing, creative power of Jesus. Whatever a person can think, see or imagine to believe will become a reality. *Jesus said to him, "If you can believe, all things are possible to him who believes"* (Mark 9:23).

When I minister healing to someone, I visually picture and see their condition in my mind's eye. Then as I lay hands on them, I look again to watch and see God's healing, restorative power entering into their diseased condition. I speak to the condition in the powerful name of Jesus. I bind the infirmity, sickness, disease or weakness, and I tell it to leave. I keep my hands on them until I hear, see or feel the power of God making them whole again. Then I rejoice in God's goodness. I ask the person healed to tell of God's healing power, to give Jesus thanks and to praise Him for His miracle-working glory.

> Miraculous signs follow those who believe in the healing power of Christ within.

God is not limited in any way, shape or form. We are the individuals who set the limits on God. The levels that we increase to prosper or decrease to diminish are determined by the level of faith (believing God for the impossible) we are willing to exercise. People are only limited if they set limits on their imagination, measure of faith and their ability to believe, see and understand. *With men this is impossible, but with God, All Things are possible* (Matthew 19:26).

God created man in His own image so that nothing would be impossible for those who believe in Him. *God created man in His own image; in the image of God He created him; male* (conscious) *and female* (subconscious)

He created them (Genesis 1:27).

Spiritual Consciousness

Apostle Paul stated that the woman or wife (the subconscious) should be subject to the man or her husband (the conscious) in everything. *Therefore, just as the Church* (subconscious) *is subject to Christ* (conscious), *so let the wives* (subconscious) *be to their own husbands* (conscious) *in everything* (Ephesians 5:24).

If we take this point of view, we can finally realize that the age-old conflict between genders really shouldn't be a male or female issue of ruling over, dominance or superiority. It is about what one thinks or says by doing the right, loving things for one's self as an individual. *So, husbands* (a conscious person) *ought to love their own wives* (subconscious) *as their own bodies; he who loves his wife* (subconscious part of himself) *loves himself* (conscious) (Ephesians 5:28).

> *Never give a place for any negative emotions to take root.*

When at rest each night, the conscious part of a person shares its ideas, thoughts and mental expressions with the subconscious part of that person. The subconscious, pictured as the womb of the wife, always willingly receives and believes what the conscious portrays, what the husband shares or relays with or ejaculates into her—his inspired thoughts, love and supporting feelings toward her.

> *Wives* (subconscious), *submit yourselves unto your own husbands* (conscious) *as unto the Lord* (Creator). *For the husband* (conscious) *is the head* (godly inspired thoughts) *of the wife* (subconscious), *even as Christ* (conscious) *is the head of the Church: and He is the savior of the body. Out of respect for Christ* (conscious), *be courteously reverent and subject to one another. Wives* (helpmate, subconscious creative womb), *understand and support your husbands* (conscious ideas and thoughts) *in ways that show your submissive service as support for Christ. The husband* (conscious) *provides leadership to his wife* (subconscious), *as the head that thinks* (consciously) *in the way Christ does as the Savior to*

His church, not by domineering but by cherishing. So, just as the Church submits to Christ (conscious) *as He exercises such leadership, wives* (subconscious) *should likewise submit in everything to their husbands* (conscious). *Husbands* (conscious) *go all out in your love for your wives* (subconscious) *exactly as Christ* (consciousness) *did for the Church—a love marked by giving, not getting that He* (conscious) *might sanctify her* (subconscious), *having cleansed her* (subconscious) *by the washing of the water with the Word.*

Christ's love makes the Church whole. That He (conscious) *might present the Church to Himself in glorious splendor, without spot or wrinkle or any such things that she* (subconscious) *might be holy and faultless. His* (conscious) *words evoke her* (subconscious) *beauty. Everything He* (the conscious) *does and says is designed to bring the best out of her,* (subconscious) *dressing her* (subconscious) *in dazzling white silk, radiant with holiness. Even so husbands* (conscious) *should love their* (subconscious) *wives as being in a sense their own bodies. He who loves his own* (subconscious) *wife loves himself* (conscious). *They're really doing themselves a favor—since the two* (conscious and subconscious) *are already 'one body' in marriage.*

No one abuses his own body, does he? No, he feeds and pampers it. That's how Christ treats us, the Church, since we are part of His body. For no man ever hated his own flesh but nourishes and carefully protects and cherishes it. Christ loves and protects the Church, because we are members of His body. Submit yourselves one to another in the fear of God. And this is why a man leaves father and mother and cherishes his (subconscious) *wife. No longer two,* (conscious and subconscious) *they become 'one flesh'. This is a huge mystery, and I don't pretend to understand it all. What is clearest to me is the way Christ treats the Church. And this provides a good picture of how each husband* (conscious) *is to treat his wife,* (subconscious) *loving himself* (conscious) *in loving her* (subconscious), *and how each wife* (subconscious) *is to honor her husband* (conscious) (Ephesians 5:21–33).

Spiritual consciousness that identifies and communes with Christ is centered on the truth of the human spirit moving as one with the Holy Spirit of God. The mystery is that these two elements, the objective (male) conscious and the subjective (female) subconscious, exist in one flesh. When they lovingly cooperate with each other in a harmonious relationship, they both serve each other's best interests.

The man (conscious) is not to lord himself over the woman (subconscious) as a dictating tyrant that dominates and controls her every thought and move. He is to be a supportive lover who protects, carefully leads, guides and instructs her (the subconscious) to understand truth so that she (the subconscious) flourishes in her own creative identity and reaches her full creative potential.

Our conscious mind is always aware of the negative, false or destructive thoughts that our subconscious is entertaining. In order to stop harming ourself and others, the thick veil of prejudicial hatred that blinds our eyes to truth must be removed. It is necessary to repent of all evil meditations. Cast down negativity, and take every vain imagination captive. If we listen to unbelievers (those with a small measure of faith) and receive their doubt-filled statements as truth, the miracle level of faith we were resting in will plummet from the heights of glory (where miracles are created) back into the carnal, natural state of our former existence.

> *Our conscious mind is always aware of the negative, false or destructive thoughts that our subconscious is entertaining.*

An unbeliever can take many forms. Unbelief can appear as a weary spouse who is ready to remarry and move on with his or her life instead caring for the terminally ill spouse. An unbeliever can be a well-intentioned but terribly misguided friend, or he or she can be a family member who is antagonistic about your prayers for healing. Doubt can appear as a priest, a denominational pastor or any other member of a traditional order of clergy that injects his or her uncertain reservations, skepticism or questions of disbelief into the subconscious heart of the one seeking healing.

All of these different forms of others' adverse, destructive distrust tap into and detract from a person's reservoir of faith; it halts, even reverses, any restorative momentum that faith was producing. Their constant interjection of doubt, as well as the questions posed by unbelief, will contain, bind and then drain, by cloaking it with a dark shroud of death, one's ability to hold onto the life energy contained in his or her healing light source. The unbeliever argues that the concrete, destructive and earthly facts about his or her beloved's diseased condition has more power to kill that person, to erase and outweigh any miracle-working, creative power of God. The doubter disputes all claims of miracles through faith and contends and reasons in his or her carnal mind that healing is not for today. Because the situation looks impossible, the doubter declares his or her unbelief to the Believer seeking to be healed.

Once one's hope is destroyed by another's carnal reasoning (and faith is systematically stripped away, denied, destroyed and removed), that person's faith weakens. The person eventually gives up hope, believes the lie that he or she has been told and finally dies. Doubt and unbelief are toxic, deadly faith, hope and life destroyers.

The precious, life-giving blood that was shed from the stripes Jesus bore heals our bruising. Christ's sword-pierced side and thorn-crowned head heals us and all of humanity. If we are sick, infirmed, diseased, halt, lame, mute or blind, we can adopt God's perfect vision of our being whole. We can walk in complete restoration. *O Lord, by these things men live; and in all these things is the life of my spirit; so, You will restore me and make me live* (Isaiah 38:16).

The sanctified imagination brings forth a renewed, Christlike mind that displays godly wisdom and leads to biblical solutions. Through God's wisdom and Word, we can tame the violence that rages around us in this chaotic society. God's wisdom brings forth peaceable answers and wise solutions.

Personal Reflection Moment

Take a moment to practice this creative healing technique.

1. Picture yourself or someone who has a physical, emotional or some other type of need.
2. Now visualize that problem being solved and re-

moved. If you or the person is sick or diseased, see yourself or that person as well, healed and whole. If you or the person is in conflict, pray to send peace into the situation or relationship. Imagine the need or desire as having been fulfilled.

3. Believe that praying and decreeing the Word of God have created the necessary wisdom, solution and power to heal, deliver and set you or the captive free.
4. Believe that your love has appropriated the creative power. Believe that it is, in fact, done! Nothing is impossible with God. You can do All Things through Christ who strengthens you.

Let Us Pray

Father, we need a fresh vision of Christ as the Holy Spirit enters to take up residence within us, as we become one with the Eternal One. Train our subconscious to use our spiritual gifts in order to gather a greater measure of revelatory insights. We want to see the imperceptible, discern the indiscernible and detect, know and respond to (with our higher spiritual senses) the obscure, concealed mysteries in the invisible realm. As we pray reverential words of actions, let spiritual doors open at a new level of consciousness.

We invite the Holy Spirit to transform us through the hearing of His voice, in dreams and visions and through the rhema Word of God. Help us to embrace God's perfect love, which casts out all fear, so that we may know we are totally accepted in the Beloved. We invite the Spirit of Truth to enter into our reality to set us free by liberating us from our diseased state. Help us to activate our sanctified imaginations to bring forth renewed, Christlike minds that display godly wisdom and lead to biblical solutions. Amen.

CHAPTER FIVE

Agree to Succeed

If we desire to grow past the limitations of man's knowledge and exceed others' knowledge, expertise and training, we must look within to personally discover our own intimacy with Christ, the supreme Teacher. When we eagerly watch for and see and listen for and hear His comings and goings, we can do whatever we observe the Christ within us challenging us to do. Then we will exceed our own expectations.

> *But I make known to you, brethren, that the gospel which was preached by me is not according to man. For I neither received it from man, nor was I taught it, but it came through the revelation of Jesus Christ* (Galatians 1:11–13).

While Jesus was living on earth, He knew that He was God. He knew He was greater than ordinary man.

> *My sheep hear My voice, and I know them, and they follow Me. And I give them eternal life, and they shall never perish; neither shall anyone snatch them out of My hand. My Father, who has given them to Me, is greater than all; and no one is able to snatch them out of My Father's hand. I and My Father are one* (John 10:27–30).

Jesus was sent to earth by His heavenly Father to redeem humanity. But Jesus also recognized that He had laid aside His divinity to walk through life as a man humbly clothed in flesh. Jesus lived modestly upon the earth. He knew that His heavenly Father was greater than He. God the Father dwelt in a higher spiritual dimension than Jesus. Because of this, Jesus would not allow people to call Him good. *So, Jesus said to him, "Why do you call Me good? No one is good but One, that is, God"* (Mark 10:18). When Jesus was in need, His consciousness looked into a higher state of being, dimension or heavenly mansion to find out what His Father (God) was doing in order to gain wisdom to solve that particular situation.

Jesus submitted to and honored His Father in heaven. Jesus prayed to His heavenly Father and asked for wisdom. He looked to see Holy Spirit visions in order to receive guidance and obtain sound judgment and answers. Jesus knew that if He moved in His own natural or earthly strengths and abilities, He would not be able to ascend high enough to attain the power necessary to be successful here on earth. After a time of visionary prayer, where Jesus could watch, see and hear what His heavenly Father was doing, Jesus and His Father became one in purposeful agreement. Through exercising His imagination in prayer, Jesus could ascend into a higher dimension to become spiritually one with His Father.

> *The art of prayer is the ability to recognize, obtain and manifest the power to be that which we desire to be rather than continually petitioning God to grant us our desires.*

Becoming one with God enables us to see as He sees and do in like manner whatever is happening in the Spirit. The Holy Spirit inspires us to do even greater things than we have been shown so that others will marvel at the power of God working through us—the power that resurrects the dead and leads others to make the decision to receive eternal life.

Jesus was dependent upon His heavenly Father for everything. The Father enjoyed showing Jesus the greater works by giving resurrection life to the dead. The person that you truly believe yourself to be cannot be defined by another person's narrow opinion of you; his or her vision is too limited and small. Your true identity can only come into being by your own personal awareness and recognition of who you are in Christ. In order to get through the door of conscious reality found in Jesus, to reach the Father's higher image of me, I must think, conceive, confess, see, imagine and believe that IAM currently who Jesus says IAM! Believing is seeing! Seeing is being! Being believes!

Jesus always consciously agreed with His Father's actions, making the same creative decrees on earth that God made in heaven. Whatever Jesus asked for or needed was already decreed and done for Jesus in heaven. Once Jesus perceived what had taken place in heaven, all He had to do was mirror those miraculous actions on earth. *Let this mind be in you which was also in Christ Jesus, who, being in the form of God, did not consider it robbery to be equal with God* (Philippians 2:6).

The Jews sought to kill Jesus not only because He broke the Sabbath tradition (by healing the infirmed, demon possessed and the halt or lame) but also because He claimed God was His Father, making Himself equal with God (see John 5:18). We draw into our consciousness what we are already conscious of being. Jesus said, "No person can come to Me unless they are conscious of My Father drawing them to Me!"

> *If two of you* (conscious and subconscious) *agree on earth it will be done for them by the Father. Again, I say to you that if two of you* (The subconscious and conscious of the Believer become one when they are aligned in agreement. And the triple cord of the Trinity—Holy Spirit, Christ Jesus and Father—are the three manifested in one God.) *heaven and earth agree concerning anything that they ask, it will be done for them by My Father in heaven* (Matthew 18:19).

This verse makes it plain that every single Believer can come into perfect alignment with the Spirit of God. The power demonstrated through this spiritual union and agreement with God guarantees that we will have our individual prayers answered.

> *In God's mighty hand is the life of every living thing and the breath of all mankind. Is it not the task of the ear to discriminate between the wise and unwise words, just as the mouth distinguishes between desirable and undesirable food? With the aged you say is wisdom, and with length of days comes understanding* (Job 12:10–12).

Heaven and earth agree as one witness. You, as the Bride of Christ, and Jesus, as the Groom, also come into a unified agreement as one witness. The Bible teaches that things are established in the eye witness of two individuals. Heaven and earth come into agreement as one witness. The subconscious and the conscious agree, as Jesus Christ in us, as the One New Man. When the spirit rules the body, the soul aligns and agrees with God's higher plans for the manifestation of the One New Man to come into being.

A husband and wife are united in a covenant marriage as one in the power of agreement. But what happens if one disagrees or desires something different? One spouse believes in healing, the other does not. One person wants to be healed and live; the other wants the battle to be over so that he or she can move on or marry someone else. Each individual who has received salvation through their confessed belief in Jesus Christ becomes one with God. You and God form a majority.

When God is for us, who can be against us? When we are united in Christ, one soldier can chase a thousand enemies off, but two that are united together as one can make ten thousand run away.

Power is the organized, coordinated knowledge and effort that is focused in a definite direction. The art of prayer is the ability to recognize, obtain and manifest the power to be that which we desire to be rather than continually petitioning God to grant us our desires.

When the masculine conscious (knowing) is joined with the feminine subconscious (creative ability), they are aligned to produce with kingdom purpose. When the conscious and subconscious are joined together in intimate communion, they become single-minded. Their womb is impregnated with fruitfulness as they come into agreement with the creative will of God.

When the masculine conscious (knowing) is joined with the feminine subconscious (creative ability), they are aligned to produce with kingdom purpose.

When these two (the conscious and subconscious) agree on a covenant promise, they are joined together, united and infused with the power of Christ's life. They are both settled in accepting the invitation to ascend. They are permeated with the wisdom that is needed to achieve a higher purpose. They have been given the spiritual understanding they need to enter into a grander destiny. This spiritual union drenches them with the power from on high to create something new. *Behold, I send the promise of My Father upon you; but tarry in the city of Jerusalem until you are endued with power from on high* (Luke 24:49).

God does not take any pleasure in our struggles, in our sacrifices or in the exerting of our physical might. In order to ascend, we must enter a higher realm of power by asking God to help our mind leave an earthly-conscious focus. To climb another rung of the ladder, we decree, see, conceive, believe and claim that we are in an increased and higher desired state of being. The Holy Spirit sends slight impressions to our subconscious. When we are conscious of their presence, we are able to see, focus on and feel them. We are able to hear the Spirit's still, small voice. We then express our response to Him through prayer, prophecy or boldly decreeing and declaring God's will in order to follow His movements, mandates and directions.

> *When these two, the conscious and subconscious, agree on a covenant promise, they are joined together, united and infused with the power of Christ's life.*

The level of confidence or unshakable conviction that we hold (being able to accomplish the end result of something) will determine the level of faith that we will place in God Almighty to help us. Stepping into God allows us to be surrounded by His image and likeness. We become one with Christ, His kingdom desires and His perfect will. When we are submerged and intermingled in His being, we take on the eternal expressions of God.

To live an abundant, fulfilling life, it is important to spend quality time carefully choosing and writing out the chief aims you have for your life. Place a written outline with highlights or bullet points of your strategic plan in a prominent place of focus. Make these goals a priority in prayer. We are able to manifest our chief aims by coming into prayerful harmony with the predominant fixed thoughts of our conscious mind. By exercising a sufficient amount of determination, meditation and contemplative prayer, we can saturate our subconscious mind until our physical body moves step-by-step toward obtaining our desired purpose in life.

Because God is not a respecter of persons, every one of us can expect to receive creative ideas, unique images, wisdom and visitations from the Spirit of God. We only need to believe, ask, seek and knock.

Let Us Pray

Dear Jesus, we submit to Your will, and we agree with Your desires for our life. We are totally dependent upon You for everything in life. We can do nothing in our own strength. We ask that You, as our supreme teacher, give us access to Your vast wisdom and revelation knowledge as we develop our spiritual intimacy with You. Help us to sense Your comings and goings in the realm of the Spirit. Gently nudge us so that we can recognize Your presence. Tune our ears to hear the whispers of Your sweet voice. Open our spiritual eyes to see into the higher dimensions so that we can see what our heavenly Father is doing. Give us the ability to look to see and understand the Holy Spirit's visions so that we can receive His guidance and obtain sound judgement. Grant us the ability to gain the wisdom and grace that is needed to live a lives that are pleasing to You. Help us take on our true identities as we recognize who You have created us to be in Christ. Amen.

CHAPTER SIX

Visiting the Potter's House

The Spirit of God is the creative force within the imagination of man. He is the inspiration that empowers the molding of the Potter's clay.

The Lord told Jeremiah, "Arise and go down to the potter's house, and there I will cause you to hear My words." Upon arriving at the potter's house, the prophet began to see. He observed that the potter had a pliable clay vessel on the wheel. The vessel the potter was making became marred in his hand, so the potter smashed it down into a lump, and he made it into a different vessel, as it seemed good to the potter (see Jeremiah 18:1–6).

God uses His loving hands to press and guide, to make or recreate, us into the image and likeness of the vessel that He has desired and predestined for each of us to become. Each individual is a different artistic design, a unique instrument, a perfect creation in the Potter's hands. It is necessary that we discover what God wants us to be and do in this world at different times and seasons. We are not to be idle and remain the same.

When the world wounds, damages, stains or mars us, we must be changed by the Potter's nail-scared hands. He lovingly reworks, heals and transforms us into a new creature. We take on His fingerprints, emerging with the touch of Christ's creative hands that have molded His characteristics and likeness into our very being. In God's presence, we are permeated with His lovely fragrance.

Feeling the authenticity of our desires (as an already fulfilled reality), and then remaining in that satisfied state, brings forth the certainty of obtaining our goals. I suggest making a lifelike model, poster, picture or graph of what you desire so that you can constantly see it before you. Every night before you go to sleep, step into the desired setting. Imagine you are within the mansion (state of being) that contains the success, entities, relationships or objectives that you desire.

> *When the world wounds, damages, stains or mars us, we must be changed by the Potter's nail-scared hands.*

Do you desire a house? Then design the house you long for on your computer, draw a sketch on paper or cut pictures out of a magazine. Do you want a job promotion? Then imagine what that position would entail, and write out the description and scope of the responsibilities and duties. Do you want to find your soulmate and get married? The lover in the Song of Songs dreamed about her soulmate during the night while she lay on her bed. She imagined who he would be and wondered what he would look like. After she had envisioned him, she took action. She went out and searched for Him until her life partner manifested.

> *One night as I lay in bed, I yearned for my lover. I yearned for him, but he did not come. So, I said to myself, "I will get up and roam the city, searching in all its streets and squares. I will search for the one I love." So, I searched everywhere but did not find him. The watchmen stopped me as they made their rounds, and I asked, "Have you seen the one I love?" Then scarcely had I left them when I found my love! I caught and held him tightly, then I brought him to my mother's house, into my mother's bed, where I had been conceived* (Song of Songs 3:1–4).

Imagine yourself as someone who is highly desired and sought after. Know and settle in your heart that you are wanted, needed, important and assured, a valuable citizen of the world. Stop clinging to your previous identity and past limitations. Change the old ways of doing things, and travel outside of the familiar territory. Launch out into the unknown, unlimited realms of life so that you can discover a much broader existence. Don't simply think of what you want to do or become; think from the realization of the fulfillment of what you want or desire to be.

> *Let not your heart be troubled; you believe in God, believe also in Me. In My Father's house are many mansions; if it were not so, I would have told you. I go to prepare a place for you. And if I go and prepare a place for you, I will come again and receive you to Myself; that where I am, there you may be also. And where I go you know, and the way you know* (John 14:1–4).

Enter into that dream state of imagination to look around. See what is available. Use the kingdom keys (ownership) to open the double doors (expanded consciousness). Crossover the threshold, and enter your Promised Land. Go into the mansion to explore everything that this spreading estate has to offer. Now move into the mansion. Take up residence, sign and own the title deed and obtain the property. Possess every detail of the ideas and identities you desire.

Go into the walk-in closet where a whole new wardrobe of mantles is waiting for you to wear. Try on the new garments, and clothe yourself in the royal robes of righteousness, wisdom and knowledge. Put on Joseph's long-sleeved, distinctive robe of the many-colored aspects of the imagination. Try on Enoch's robe of intimacy, and walk with God. Become the all different attributes and characteristics, and wear the expressions of the numerous garments that are available to you.

Each garment has its boundary of limitations as well as its specific strengths and broadening assets that no other garment possesses. We learn how to clothe ourself in Christ by putting on and taking off certain mantles at the right time. This level of discernment will equip us to live in Christ, move in the Holy Spirit and have our being in a current, fashionable expression of Christ's will.

Think higher thoughts from your new mansion. Believe you are there. Imagine your goals are accomplished, and remain present in that state of belief. Let the real self of your imagination know that you are at hand, having moved beyond to take up residence.

The places and mansions that we create and see in our imagination cause us to experience profound events for the first time. This practice causes us to be proficient in the exercise of the desire to remain there in a higher place, and it causes us to experience a broader dimension so that we become familiar with these encounters.

Every time we open a door to enter in, crossing over a threshold to possess a territory, new dimension, different state of being or spacious mansion in God, we must realize that it is already fully furnished and complete. The Bible states that our gifts will make room for us to advance and prosper before great men (see Proverbs 18:16).

Jesus instructed the people in the priest's house to make room. For the presence of His miracle, healing gift of resurrection power, Jesus put the doubters, grievers and unbelieving out to conquer death and fill her body with life. *He said, "Go away. The girl is not dead but sleeping." And they ridiculed Him* (Matthew 9:24).

Walking within God empowers us to flow in the omnipresent power of the Lord, who dwells, owns and has taken possession of everything that is present.

We can be sure that when we transition from one state or place to another, *He will show you a large upper room, furnished and prepared; there made ready for us* (Mark 14:15).

Walking within God empowers us to flow in the omnipresent power of the Lord, who dwells, owns and has taken possession of everything that is present. Having the fullness of God present, there is not any room for an idol to enter in, reside or be set up in that holy place. A lesser power cannot overcome you, for God, the greatest power in the universe, is living in and through you.

> *The Philistines took the Ark chest, the dwelling place of the One True God. They brought the Ark into the house of their god Dagon and set it by the idol Dagon. And when the people of Ashdod arose early in the morning, there was Dagon, fallen on its face to the earth as if he were worshipping before the covenant Ark of the Eternal LORD. So, they took Dagon and set it up in its proper place again. And when they arose early the next morning, there was Dagon, fallen on its face to the*

> *ground before the Ark of the LORD. The head of Dagon and both the palms of its hands were broken off and lying across the threshold; only Dagon's torso was left of it. Therefore, neither the priests of Dagon nor any who come into Dagon's house tread on the threshold of Dagon in Ashdod to this day. But the hand of the Eternal LORD was heavy with punishment on the people of Ashdod, and He ravaged them and struck them with painful tumorous growths, both Ashdod and its territory. And when the men of Ashdod saw how they had been cursed, they said, "The Ark of the God of Israel must not remain here with us, for His hand is harsh, and His judgments are toward us and Dagon our god"* (1 Samuel 5:2–7).

Our sustained imagination causes us to be conformed to the reality of the new life we desire. If we stay focused on that higher state until we fall asleep in that dimension of being in time, we will be able to obtain and sustain that present desire in our waking life. The abundant life that is promised to us comes when we recognize God is the Creator who lives within our sanctified, controlled and vivid imagination. Our life is but a shadow of the things to come, yet within the dimensions of our own heart, we hold heaven and earth.

It is important that we never close our mind to the probability of the impossible becoming possible. We need to embrace our highest potential, and then we must pray to make detailed plans to achieve it. Stop looking for reasons to fail or to be offended by people and situations. Open your mind to innovative experiences. Become intrigued with the unknown. Search out, discover and explore what seem to be different views. They are not really new. They have always been in God even though they are a fresh and contemporary way of seeing things. They differ from the way we currently think or believe. Keep in mind that a placebo is a convincing belief in which we place our faith in order to receive a healing cure.

We need to embrace our highest potential, and then we must make detailed plans to achieve it.

Attachments bring weighted limitations and restrictions. Bonds set boundaries that are defined by the length of the leash or sphere that our tether allows us to explore. Therefore, it is obvious that we should not define our happiness according to the actions and responses of others. Be open to all godly things. Be willing to detach yourself from every earthly asset and accessory. By seeking the Kingdom of God first, we learn how to invest everything that we are and all that we own into advancing His Kingdom within us.

We cannot share love with another person if love is not within our heart. Our constant seeking of someone to love but never finding them proves that we have not developed a giving, supportive, sacrificial and loving nature within our heart. We cannot give to another what we do not own or currently possess, what we have working in our character (for example, love in our heart). We will only be able to give out that which we are, currently possess or have at our disposal. Without love, our personality will display contempt, project anger and exude a critical nature that is full of judgmental statements. For out of the abundance of the heart, the mouth speaks.

Without love, our personality will display contempt, project anger and exude a critical nature that is full of judgmental statements.

To be born again, we must first determine who we are currently in our carnal nature. Once we are able to distinguish what is not of our spirit nature, we must repent and desire to change. We must die to our old individual by a spiritual rebirth into Christ in order to become a life-giving being who is a positive, creative, life-speaking spirit.

The true inner image of a man will form and project that spoken truth in his outer world for people to see, hear and believe. The inner beauty of peace will draw an outer manifestation of tranquility, joy and prosperity. On the other hand, deceitful actions that stem from the mistrust of others will draw ignoble circumstances and selfish people into our realm.

> *We don't get wormy apples off a healthy tree, nor good apples off a diseased tree. The health of the apple foretells the health of the tree. Out of the virtue that is stored up in our hearts good and upright people will produce good fruit. We must begin with our own life-giving lives. It's who we are, not what we say and do, that counts. Our true being brims over into true*

> *words and deeds. But out of the evil hidden in our hearts we produce what is evil. For the overflow of what has been stored in our heart will be seen by our fruit, and will be heard in our words* (Luke 6:45).

Personal Reflection Moment

Take time to observe your own thoughts and actions. Listen to hear the internal conversations that are being held in the privacy of your heart (imagination).

1. Are the words, thoughts and actions noble or ignoble?
2. Are your words gentle, kind and full of life with well wishes? Or are the thoughts and words of your heart destructive, jealous, limiting, selfish, intolerant and full of hate and destruction?

To experience a rebirth into who we want to be, we must first recognize who we truly are in secret. We must be aware of our wanton, fleshly, selfish reactions. We then need to set our aim to consciously change into a higher spiritual, ideal self. Awaken each morning with this new image or state of being—born again into a kind, loving and generous person. Keep that persona clearly focused in the mind.

The selfish prodigal son who left home said, "Give me my inheritance!" The father said to his other son who stayed at home to serve him, "All that I have is thine." In the Father's house, there is access to an abundance of everything we need. This wealth flows into an addition that increases and multiplies into an excess of fullness that overflows into every area of life.

> *When we realize that it is our continual projection of the poverty mentality that has created our lack in life, we will repent.*

In order for us to access the unlimited prosperity found in the Father's mansions, we must separate ourself from our long-term expected norms, routine reactions and the pigpen to which we habitually return. When we realize that it is our continual projection of the poverty mentality that has created our lack in life, we will repent. I will elaborate more on this in a following chapter.

By taking on a higher conscious level of thought and action, we ascend out of the pit of condemnation. We move into a place where we are able to partake of the fatted calf, wear a new garment and bear a golden ring as we exercise our covenant authority in Christ. God's grace is sufficient for each one of us, and His power is made manifest in and through our weaknesses. The way each of us measures right and wrong is a personal matter that is determined by the way we believe and think about a certain thing.

> *I know and am convinced, fully persuaded as one in the Lord Jesus, that nothing is forbidden as essentially unclean, defiled and unholy in itself. But nonetheless, it is unclean, defiled and unholy to anyone who thinks it is unclean* (Romans 14:14).

Personal Reflection Moment

As a representation of a life-giving spirit, one should ask, "How may I serve people, God and my country? What can I give to the world?" Ask not what God, country or people can do for you. Ask what you can do for them. We must continually inventory who we are and examine what is within our heart so that we may reflect God's divine nature, not our carnal nature.

1. Are you able to bless and love your enemies while they curse, abuse and use you?
2. How much love, compassion, mercy or grace do you have and show toward yourself and others?

What we sow to others, good or evil, we will also reap from others (reference to A Call to Destiny in Volume III).

There is not any justified reason to hold resentments toward or to place blame on another. Holding others at blame produces hostile anger and unforgiveness. This causes a backup of the bitterness of guile that produces gallstones, which negatively affects and blocks the gallbladder's ability to flow. If we are brutally honest with ourself, we will discover that most of our woes are due to our own self-sabotaging thoughts, unforgiveness and wrongful actions.

Learn to forgive quickly those who borrowed the widow's hard-earned retirement money with the promise to repay her with more interest than the bank offered but never made good on their promise. Forgive those who craftily stole from you, lied to you, defrauded you or were cruel in their rejection of you. Forgive those who have betrayed, divorced, cheated on or abused you. If you continue to choose to maintain a state of bitterness and unforgiveness, it will cause a spiritual dullness, deafness and blindness. Bitterness draws a spirit of failure, lack, poverty, dis-ease and death. These effects are too high of a price to pay in order to get even with someone who has caused you grief.

By taking responsibility for our fleeting thoughts, we can regulate them in order to change and redirect our actions. To do this, you must first repent and forgive yourself for any inappropriate, critical, judgmental or limiting thoughts you have entertained about yourself or others. Now love yourself. Begin to let go, and move forward into God's steadfast grace. Always send the power of love to people in response to their hate. There are no justified reasons to maintain any hatred toward yourself or others.

If you continue to choose to maintain a state of bitterness and unforgiveness, it will cause a spiritual dullness, deafness and blindness.

Never enter into or come under the influence of a negative spirit, bad attitude or limiting thought pattern. Instead, always respond in God's power, bestowing His love and great grace to people and giving honor where honor is due. Since all people are created in the image of God, even the most vile reprobate or deprived person is due a small measure of honor. Stay out of the shadows of resentment. Renounce the toxic poison of bitterness. Do not entertain, even for a minute, any level of unforgiveness. When our words are evil, envious and full of jealousy, we proudly justify and defend our own failures while we criticize and condemn the failures and distresses of others.

Let Us Pray

Spirit of God, You are the creative force within my being. You are the Potter, and IAM the marred clay vessel in Your skilled, loving, nail-scarred hands. Help me to be submitted to You, pliable and willing to be molded into a different vessel as it seems good to You. Press, shape and guide me, and recreate me according to Your blueprints, image and likeness. Give me a fresh vision of who IAM called to be in You. Let me picture the scope of the responsibilities and duties You have assigned for me to accomplish in life. Thank you that Your desire is toward me. Help me to have to confidence in You so that I can launch out into the unknown. Help me to advance past my physical limitations in order to discover my existence in Your boundless Spirit. Teach me how to use the keys of the Kingdom so that I can open the double doors of Your blessings. Help me to move from my present state of being into a higher mansion in Your Father's house. Give me the ability to slay every idol that attempts to set itself up in Your place. Deliver me from being a selfish prodigal who is only concerned about my inheritance. Restore me to my right mind, and give me the mind of Christ. Amen.

CHAPTER SEVEN

Deadly Snake Bites

No one dies from a snake's bite! Death comes from the necrotic venom released from a venomous snake's fangs upon contact. The venom is injected into the bloodstream that spreads the poisonous toxins throughout the body. It is the snake's toxic venom that circulates within its victim's blood system and causes the harmful destruction. The snake's venom stuns, paralyzes and destroys the victim's vital organs. It is the venom that causes the necrosis of the cells in the organs' tissue, which executes the final blow and carries out a painfully slow, violent death sentence. In the same regard, venomous thoughts and poisonous, hate-filled words will kill you if they are not stopped with the antivenins of love, mercy, grace and forgiveness.

You cannot solve a critical current or past problem with the same negative mindset that created the adversity. It is imperative and wise that you acknowledge and confess when you make a mistake due to a lack of knowledge or poor choices. Once you have repented and asked for forgiveness, you are able to shift and lift into a higher plain of thought. Continue to focus on God's desires by embracing His higher ways, thoughts and plans. Place your full attention on magnifying and worshipping God in a peaceful atmosphere of praise.

Stop focusing your attention on the problem; this practice only causes the problem to grow. Repent and pray for God's wisdom. Give up your personal past. Stop rejecting the grand, ingenious thoughts and ideas that God is giving you. Let the greatness of Christ emerge from within your imagination. Give His magnificent plans and desires expression in your life. In order to change for the positive, it is important to stop collecting, bagging, classifying and carrying around all of your prior mistakes. Never bond with your history of failure by hauling it around with you as your personal baggage. Mistakes are only temporary setbacks if you learn to grow from them.

Every day begins with the darkness of night, for that is when we see the bright stars that light us up with the hope of a new day dawning. Awake to a new day, clean the slate, and start fresh. Break and renounce old, mournful patterns. Refuse to strain your neck by focusing on the wake behind the boat. Place both oars in the water, climb out of the pit, change direction, and move forward to break out of the former patterns. Pull yourself together. It will take all of your strength to break yourself out of a cycle of limited influence. With all of your might, begin to row toward the dawning of the bright and rising sun. The horizon is vast and beautiful. Propel yourself headlong into the broad expanse of an unlimited future.

Be at peace. Enter into rest. Place your trust in God. The Spirit of Truth arises in the heart of your imagination to give you rest by leading and guiding you into all truth! *However, when He, the Spirit of truth, has come, He will guide you into all truth; for He will not speak on His own authority, but whatever He hears He will speak; and He will tell you things to come* (John 16:13).

If you have a disease or sickness, you must take responsibility for your weakened condition. At times, disease is the result of destructive choices one has made. Unforgiveness issues are an invitation for base, low spiritual frequencies to take up residence within your body. Their evil or demonic presence significantly slows down the healthy vibrations or pulse within the body. These virulent entities place a great deal of undo stress and strain on every bodily function and system. If the malevolent spirits are not bound, renounced and cast out of their host's body, one or more of the organs they inhabit will start to weaken, fail or stop functioning.

Let the greatness of Christ emerge from within your imagination.

Evil thoughts and actions will draw all manner of evil beings into your conscious mind, body, circumstances and environment. If you become steadfast in your evil thoughts of harm toward yourself or others, all living creatures will stop feeling safe in your presence. But if you move in a loving spirit, all living creatures will stop fearing you, and they will be drawn into your sphere in order to feel love and peaceful tranquility.

If I take responsibility for my actions, I can change them. I can repent of my wrong thoughts, behaviors or dealings, move on and receive my deliverance and healing. Always send love in response to hate, and always choose to bless instead of casting a curse. Return a soft answer to wrath and rage. Continue to release more love toward others. Whether a person is doing us good or harm, they are still being used by God to help mold us into a better person.

> *Never bond with your history of failure by hauling it around with you as your personal baggage.*

It is the quality of choices we make that determines the positive harmony or the negative, static outcomes we experience. The embracing of the silence found in prayer and meditation on God's Word, principles and precepts brings forth the best answers to life's hard or difficult questions. When we choose to identify with the highest possible form of Christ in our conscious being, the imagination locks our faith into that state. Faith connects us to God. When we see ourself with the eyes of faith, we are conscious of the power of Christ dwelling within. It is God that empowers us to manifest the virtues of what we have imagined ourself to be.

Intentionally release your toxic history of pain. Stop carrying harmful baggage around with you. Do not let the temporary failures, setbacks and disappointments you have endured define you. Never let what others say about you define your outlook on yourself or on life. Believe what God says about you. He created you, and He has the owner's manual. Ask God who He says you are, and then believe His words. Listen to what God says about you. Allow His power and grace to define your character. Never believe the lies of the enemy; he will always try to marginalize your potential. When you were born, the enemy of your soul said, "Make them think that they are invisible, that no one sees them, that no one cares." But what your spirit heard was, "With Christ, you are invincible!"

Take one final look at the waves in the wake of your destructive history. Decide to embrace the good and bad decisions of the past by acknowledging and owning them. Then choose to forgive yourself and others for every mistake, sin and offense. Watch as the tumultuous waves of pain begin to dissipate. Let go of all of the physical, mental and emotional trauma and turmoil. Allow the waters of life to flow back into a peaceful, tranquil, still sheet. Lean over, gaze into the clear reflection of the water and see the beautiful image of your newly-healed identity in the face that is looking back at you.

Wisdom is avoiding the negative thoughts of shame, guilt, failure, fear, anger and anxiety that steal your creative power and God consciousness.

To solve problems, you have to renew your mind with the life-giving Spirit of the Word of God. It is the Spirit of God the Father who gives us the gift of life and draws us to Jesus. Sheer willpower cannot make anything happen. No one can solve a problem with the same mindset, choices, actions and identity that created it.

True love loves people for who they really are, not for who we desire them to become in the future. Therefore, start acting as if you are already the person you want to become. Wisdom is avoiding the negative thoughts of shame, guilt, failure, fear, anger and anxiety that steal your creative power and your Christ consciousness that God is love. Overcome obstacles by exercising great faith, not by slinking (cloaked in fear) around things. Focus on the good news that a new day brings, not on the lies that cause worry and anxiety. The thoughts you think about and focus upon will be magnified and expanded until they take over your life. Therefore, let your thoughts be life-giving, not venomous and deadly.

Let Us Pray

Dear Holy Spirit, I ask that You permeate every fiber of my being. Deliver me from the poisonous, toxic words of others. Renew my mind so that it only thinks on those things that are pure, holy, trustworthy and full of grace. Help me to embrace Your higher thoughts and ways. Place my attention on Your goodness and mercy. I need Your wisdom to emerge within me. I repent of carrying around the baggage of past mistakes. Help me to stop focusing on my failures. Help me see my mistakes as temporary setbacks, not death sentences, that have worked a new strength within me and have caused me to grow in my trust of You. Give me a fresh vision that will empower me to focus on a prosperous, unlimited future. I embrace Your perfect peace, and I enter into a place of rest in You. I repent of all of my wrong thoughts and actions. I release my toxic emotions into Your hands. I choose to receive Your healing and deliverance from my past. Help me to return love for hate and blessings for curses. I choose to love people for who they are, not for who I want them to be. Amen.

CHAPTER EIGHT

Fear is the Enemy!

Fear is rooted in selfishness that reasons we can take better care of ourself than God can. Fear is false faith that causes us to believe a lie. If we believe a lie about ourself, it will eventually manifest as a negative harmful reality in our life. Even though that lie is false, if we trust in it and place our full, persistent confidence in it, we will believe it as truth. That lie will then produce fear. Fear causes us to seize control when it is not ours to take.

Because we are not free to make our own choices when we are controlled by others, it causes anger to rise within us. When we feel trapped by emotional control or in a place of physical bondage, it can cause rage to explode into a murderous desire. When people are controlled by someone else or something, their spirit is broken, their personality is squashed and their soul goes into a hopeless bondage. Their health deteriorates, and their body eventually dies. The only real obstacles we encounter are the negative, fearful mental images that we create within our own mind. Man is not born with fear. The God of Love has given us His love, power and a sound mind.

Moses was the meekest man on earth during his time period; however, his anger kept him from entering the Promised Land. The things we fear are learned, inflicted on us from others or developed through bad experiences. We often inherit these unreasonable fears from people who try to exercise excessive authority over us. We learn to fear during our formative years often because of the negative influences of dominating parents, jealous siblings or other relatives, fickle friends or insecure teachers. Most people attempt to dominate others by injecting their controlling, fearful thoughts into others' conscious thoughts.

The prosperous CEO or businessperson who keeps confessing to his board of directors, "Our good fortune cannot continue forever!" is prophesying the end to his own success. His fearful business outlook draws failure into the corporation. His demise comes due to the lack of a prosperous vision. Instead of indulging fear or stating a false truth, learn to stare fear in the face until it backs down, disappears and fades away. Focusing on a negative idea or toxic thought, even for a minute, causes it to form, take shape and gain momentum.

Champions develop a strong and disciplined mind so that negative thoughts cannot continue to manifest. A sound, calm mind that is fixed on God's peace easily overcomes all mental suggestions of fear. Focusing on the positive will remove every obstacle from their path. *I sought the Lord, and He heard me, and delivered me from all my fears* (Psalm 34:40). Mental discipline causes their anointing to overflow and wash out the narrow boundaries caused by man-made restrictions. A sound mind based in the truth of the Word of God is like a river surging past its limitations, raging on through uncharted territories on the behalf of other people.

Fear is rooted in selfishness that reasons we can take better care of ourself than God can.

David and Goliath

David had to face off the giant Goliath in the Valley of Elah, not on a beautiful mountaintop. It is easy to spot and confront a giant because they are such enormous, loud targets. Giant obstacles fall easily when they are acknowledged, met and tackled in the faith of God. Huge giants don't back down, hide, disappear or leave their territory without being threatened, confronted and defied. Gigantic giants remain an antagonistic stronghold until they are provoked, opposed and defeated face-to-face.

If you are facing a giant in your life, confess out loud, "I am not afraid of giants! I am a brave, champion giant slayer! The bigger the giants are in my life, the harder they will fall when I cut off their head with their own sword." Being more than a conqueror means that the giants of yesterday no longer show up to the battle for fear that their head will roll when our sword severs it from their body.

When God changes our name, identity and reputation, we are transformed from a person who used to be fearful—who used to back down, hide, quit or run away—into a courageous giant slayer! We become a formidable force to be reckoned with! Instead of fearing the giants who used to keep us out of our Promised Land, we eagerly hunt them down and destroy them just for the sport of it. Make it a practice to uproot every negative or fear-based thought, and replace each one of them with constructive, life-giving verses from Scripture. God's transformation process utilizes the trained attention of our controlled imagination that is firmly focused on the objective that it expects to obtain.

Fear causes failure, poverty and death. However, if our confidence is secure in God, we have the measure of faith that is necessary to move mountains. Refuse to agree with negative statements that are based in fear. Others' negative, threatening statements do not have the power to upset us unless we give them that power and ability. Never turn your back and run away from fear. If you do, it will continue to pursue you. Instead, look fear square in the face, stare it down, back it off and destroy it.

Pray in faith, prophesy great things and decree the opposite statement of what fear is trying to project into your life. By submitting your heartfelt beliefs and desires to the will of God, the reality of your new identity (being in the IAM part of the One New Man in God) causes you to assume a higher, loving concept of yourself. Love conquers all fear. Learn to laugh in the face of fear.

Pray in faith, prophesy great things and decree the opposite statement of what fear is trying to project into your life.

Decree the life-giving Word of God until it is written upon the tablet of your heart. Expect to obtain the absolute best out of life. When we always expect the finest, we will draw the very best life has to offer into our sphere of influence. In order to remove fear from your life, focus on substituting fear with more faith. Focus on filling your life with positive, good things that produce peace and happiness.

Invite the light of God to increase until the power of God's abiding presence crowds out any dark place for fear to hide. Once this higher concept is believed, visualized and felt, we learn to rest in the Lord. We behave differently when we are manifesting the future vision of ourself. We learn to enjoy overcoming the challenges that are found in the adventures we had once only hoped for.

Jesus is the Passover Door. When we seek, find, knock on and open this door, we are given the necessary power of love and faith to escape from fear. Jesus is our access door to the faith of God. Jesus delivers us from the wilderness death of aimless wandering. Jesus is the door that gives us entrance into our Promised Land. Jesus is the way, the truth and the life path that leads to everything we want, need or desire.

The Revelation 4:1–3 door remains open in heaven. The voice of the trumpet has spoken: "Come up here into the throne room of My Spirit, and I will show you what must take place after these things." Whenever we enter a different spiritual door in Jesus, we must wisely choose the more complex, superior direction that we will go. Sadly, most people choose to go back into the familiar past by retracing their every day, recurring steps. Instead of overcoming, prospering and learning how to triumph in virgin territory, they become stuck (reliving their bygone history of failures) and paralyzed by fears.

If we choose to remain behind the door of the present, we remain safe and secure in our current timeframe, but while living in the habitual familiar, we do not grow, ascend or advance.

If we choose to remain behind the door of the present, we remain safe and secure in our current timeframe, but while living in the habitual familiar, we do not grow, ascend or advance. Because we have refused to take the necessary risks to increase our measure of faith, we stagnate and remain the same typical, common person. However, if we choose to boldly advance through the double doors of access that leads into our eternal future, we instantly gain the revelation knowledge that is necessary to be transformed into the image of Christ. We become an extraordinary (new) creature who is aligned with the One New Man.

> *For you have acquired new creation life which is continually being renewed into the likeness of the One who created you; giving you the full revelation of God. In this new creation life, your nationality makes no difference, or your ethnicity, education, or economic status—they matter nothing. For it is Christ that means everything as He lives in every one of us* (Colossians 3:10 11)*!*

When fear is knocking at the door of your heart, let your faith in God arise. Then answer fear in the overcoming power of Christ's faith. Whenever I am afraid, I will put my trust and all of my faith in Christ (see Psalm 56:3).

Let Us Pray

Dear Jesus, I know that I was not born with fear. You have not given me a spirit of fear, failure, poverty or death but of love and power. Thank you for giving me a free will so that I can make my own choices in life. Please forgive me for the times I have allowed others to control me. I ask You to heal me of a broken spirit. Restore my hope in You, and grant me a prosperous future. Heal the health of my body, soul and spirit. Thank you for giving me Your undying love and power, and thank You for giving me a sound mind.

Give me the grace to overcome the fears that took root in me during my formative years. Help me overcome the hurtful words of my jealous siblings, dominating relatives, fickle friends and insecure teachers. Empower me to develop a strong, disciplined mind that continually thinks on Your peace and the truth that is found in Your Word. Give me the skills that are necessary to cut the head off of every giant who would dare raise its ugly head. Endow me with the power to wield Your two-edged sword of truth so that I can slay every fear that would try to keep me out of my Promised Land. Help me to continue to move forward. Support me in my efforts to conquer every challenge. Lend me Your great courage to face and never run away from the things I fear. Amen.

CHAPTER NINE

Creative Miracles

The character of God authorizes us to prophetically pray, decree and declare God's Kingdom to come into our life. We become the vehicles that draw the manifestation of God's presence into the earth's atmosphere. Christ manifests His power through salvation, deliverance, healing and the creative miracle realms being demonstrated in people's lives. Experimenting with the creative realms of God's miracle provision (through gaining the understanding of the ways of God) will bring us untold godly wisdom, knowledge, influence, abundance, riches and prosperity.

Allow me to paraphrase Mark 35:35–43:

> Jesus had just healed the man with legions of demons and a woman who had an issue of blood flowing from her body for twelve years. Jesus was still speaking when some came from the ruler of the synagogue's house. They said to Jairus, "Your daughter has died. Why bother and distress the Teacher any further?" Jesus overheard them, but He ignored their comments. Jesus spoke hope to Jairus, "Do not be alarmed or allow fear to strike and seize your heart; only keep on believing."
>
> Jesus then set an atmosphere of faith. Jesus did not allow any unbelievers in the crowd to accompany Him. Jesus only permitted Peter, James and John, the brother of James.

> He only allowed Believers who were full of faith to travel with Him to heal, restore and raise the little girl from the clutches of death.
>
> When Jesus and His team of Believers arrived at the house of the ruler of the synagogue, Jesus carefully looked at the situation with spiritual understanding. The house was full of tumult, doubt, fear, unbelief, weeping and loud wailing. When Jesus walked into this dark atmosphere of death, He said to the unbelievers, "Why do you make such an uproar and weep? The little girl is not dead but is sleeping."
>
> The detractors laughed at Jesus and angrily mocked His statement of faith, jeering at Him. Jesus again responded to unbelief by setting up a miracle atmosphere that was conducive for faith to rule. He put all the mourners out of the child's bedroom, and He only allowed the child's father, mother and the three Believers who were with Him to come into where the little girl was lying.
>
> Gripping her firmly by the hand, Jesus said to her, "Talitha cumi (little girl), I say to you, arise from the sleep of death!" The miracle light of faith instantly entered into the twelve-year-old girl's body. She resurrected, got up and started walking around—and they were utterly astonished and overcome with amazement. Jesus gave a strict command and warned them that no one should know this, and He told them to give her some food to eat.

Miracles always exist and travel in a much higher realm of the Spirit. Miracles are manifested at an accelerated or quickened rate of speed. They violate the natural laws by drawing glory matter that was not currently present a second ago into a person, place or thing. Miracles manifest by recreating something that was already present but was sick, diseased or lacking. Whatever we can see, believe and focus on obtaining, we can be or have! The places we go to see and experience in our imagination become ours when we believe them as a reality and stake a claim to them. Wherever the soles of our feet may travel and tread upon (the same as Joshua taking possession of Jericho), God has already given unto us (see Joshua 1:3).

The story of Joshua gives us the victory formula to move forward (to be successful) by breaking down walls and moving to take virgin territory, regardless of the obstacles. Joshua did this by simply placing his feet on new property. Joshua employed Rahab, the prostitute, even though to the natural mind she was the most unlikely candidate to help him conquer an impenetrable wall. Unlikely, yes! But Rahab, the harlot, had the unique skill sets that were needed to manipulate the situation in order to protect the Israeli spies. We can become like Joshua by believing the promises of God and by setting our feet firmly upon the property or place we desire in our imagination. Stepping into destiny empowers us to take down walls that keep us from possessing Jericho, which is our walled off, seemingly impossible desired objective.

> *Experimenting with the creative realms of God's miracle provision, through gaining the understanding of the ways of God, will bring us untold godly wisdom, knowledge, influence, abundance, riches and prosperity.*

Rahab represents thinking outside the box, incorporating those with different views and skill sets and embracing the unusual to do whatever is necessary to spy out the land of promises in the secret place in order to gain the revelation needed to break through. A prostitute gives everything that is asked of her in service in order to obtain the fee she desires for her focused time. She does not question whether she is physically capable or morally correct. When we are conscious of visualizing, seeing, conceiving, birthing and obtaining our future goals, every frontier will become our present state of being.

The seven blasts of the trumpets represent the duration of seven days (the number of fullness and God's perfection) that transpired as Joshua entered into a time of his conscious mind, resting in a hidden place of peaceful expectancy. Joshua remained determined in that imaginative place until his visionary desire was conceived, birthed and then physically accomplished. Joshua's steadfast knowing that he would be successful caused the walls of Jericho to fall with seven mighty trumpet blasts.

The expanded vision granted to us by our imagination gives us the title deed to what we believe and see. Declarative prayer draws that which we have imagined in the realm of the Spirit into our sphere of authority so that we can acquire, take ownership of and possess the very things that we desire.

The presence of God is always waiting for us to increase, prosper, enlarge and succeed at a much greater degree. To become more, we must ascend into the higher God-conscious reality. When we journey further into God, beyond the natural realms of limitations, we gain the wisdom that is necessary to manifest God's power in a superior manner and measure.

Personal Reflection Moment

1. Determine and define your goal without being caught up with how you will manifest your objectives. Take a minute to close your natural eyes. Now open your spiritual eyes of vision to imagine the exact dimension of your expectation. See a clear picture of yourself in a new place of obtaining favor in a new state of being.
2. Take your focused attention off the Jericho wall (person, belief or obstacle) that is obstructing your advancement. At present, place your entire focus on your specific goal or desired objective.
3. Now believe it is possible to see with your spiritual eyes and feel with your spirit that you have already placed your feet upon the new territory that your heart desires.
4. Remain in this elevated sphere of imagination until you are conscious of having already captured your intended desire as a reality. As the walls of opposition fall, open your eyes to see that you are able to bring your new conscious state of reality back with you into the natural realm of victory.

First and foremost, it is very important to live a virtuous life that believes in, loves, trusts and serves God. When we place God first in our life, whatever we can desire, imagine and believe is true about God will become possible as a manifested reality for us. We receive things from God depending upon the measure of faith we place in Him. But more importantly, we change things depending upon the measure of the faith of God we possess. The woman with the issue of blood pressed through the crowd in order to touch Jesus' robe.

> *Jesus felt healing power surge through Him when she touched Him in faith to receive her healing. Jesus responded to her faith, "Beloved daughter, your faith in Me has released your healing. You may go with My peace"* (Luke 8:46–48).

Times of focused meditation on the ways of God give us fresh understanding of how to establish the visions we see in the imagination of our mind's eye. Thinking from a particular mansion and seeing the end result in that state of being is a creative principle that is only found in that place. When we are centered in Christ, we see things that are already completed and finished in Him. This empowers our imagination to retrieve and sustain its focus upon visions that foretell the outcomes of the future.

> When we journey further into God, beyond the natural realms of limitations, we gain the wisdom that is necessary to manifest God's power in a superior manner and measure.

Focused prayer brings the indiscernible into clarity in our present consciousness. The dimensions we travel to in our imagination become ours when we invest in what has already been given to us.

> *For whoever has spiritual knowledge of mysteries, to him more wisdom and understanding will be given and he will be furnished richly so that he will have abundance; but from him who has not, even what he has will be taken away* (Matthew 13:12).

God moves through the measure of the knowledge of Christ's awakened, resident power (that we have acquired) working within us. An awakened imagination that is centered in Christ has the power to create beauty, heal and work miracles by destroying the unlovely. However, if you focus on the destructive riots and storms of life and agree with fear or identify yourself with any unpleasant, objectionable state, you will deteriorate until you find yourself descending into that dark abbess. We must carefully govern all of our thoughts, ideas and what we feel is true at all times.

> *Jesus ministered from place to place, He taught in the synagogues, preaching the hope of the kingdom realm and healing every kind of sickness and disease among the people. His fame spread everywhere! Huge crowds of people streamed up hills to bring the lame, blind, deformed, mute and many other people who were in pain and suffering with every kind of illness to Jesus and laid at His feet for their healing—epileptics, paralytics, and those tormented by demonic powers were all set free. Everyone who was brought to Jesus was healed* (Matthew 4:23–24; 15:30)*!*

Doctors may give reports of death: your condition is terminal; your disease is rare, so it has no cellular markers to treat or target; it is too difficult to heal; I'm sorry, but you have a short life expectancy. Regardless of what diagnosis is given, if you receive (agree with) the report as truth, you feed your subconscious with the feelings of fear, doubt and unbelief. Because you do not understand the healing process, your subconscious will automatically erect barriers that will prevent your own healing. This occurs even if you receive another's sympathy or feel self-pity or sorrow for yourself. Ignorance of the ways of God seals your fate.

> An awakened imagination that is centered in Christ has the power to create beauty, to heal and to work miracles by destroying the unlovely.

> *But let him ask in faith, with no doubting, for he who doubts is like a wave of the sea driven and tossed by the wind. For let not man suppose that he will receive anything from the Lord; he is a double-minded man, unstable in all his ways* (James 1:6–8).

If we expect to continue to grow in spiritual maturity, we must search out, find and continually access a new dimension of God. Allow the healing words you've heard from Me to live in you and make them a model for life as your faith and love for the Anointed One grows even more (2 Timothy 1:13).

The revelation knowledge of God that we currently possess must always be expanding, growing and proceeding into the vast, unlimited expanses of God. The things that we believe and accept as truth, whether they are true or false, clothe us. In order for us to ascend into a higher realm of truth, we must take off the restrictive garments and trappings that thither us to a lower level.

> *The Believer must continually bring healing to lepers and to those who are sick, and make it our habit to break off the demonic presence from people, and raise the dead back to life. Freely we have received the power of the kingdom, so freely release it to others* (Matthew 10:8).

Let Us Pray

Heavenly Father, thank you for giving us the authority to prophetically pray, decree and declare that Your Kingdom come and manifest in the earth today! By Your grace, we can access the miracle provisions of God's wisdom to gain His divine knowledge, to exercise our spiritual influence in order to gain His abundant riches and prosperity. Thank you that Christ's power to overcome death lives within us. Whatever we can see, believe and maintain our faith focus upon, we can obtain, be or have! Wherever the soles of our feet tread, You have already given unto us. Thank you for granting us with new vision in our imaginations so that we can see and decree and be everything You desire for us to be. Help us steward the measure of revelation knowledge that we currently possess. Holy Spirit, come expand, grow and process us so that our understanding of You will manifest throughout the unlimited expanses of eternity. Amen.

CHAPTER TEN

Prophecy

Seeing four-dimensionally is seeing prophetically. Once the Holy Spirit reveals the destiny of a person to a prophet, the prophet can release a sure sound of prophecy. Prophetic words contain a powerful creative light that initiates a spiritual movement (a realignment and coming together of a foundational structure) of bones, muscles, sinew and a new wineskin covering. Prophecy, when it is spoken as Holy Spirit commands, is the spiritual life breath that is breathed into another's dry (three-dimensional) bones. *For He whom God has sent speaks the words of God, for God does not give the Spirit by measure* (John 3:34). There are no restrictive limits placed on the prophet's spirit in the immeasurable fourth dimension.

Prophecy creates a sure vibratory sound that resonates with a higher truth that causes things to shake, rattle and roll together into a new form of alignment or support structure. Prophetic decrees establish the structure by adding muscles, sinew and covering to the body with flesh that causes the person to gain strength with forward momentum and liberty of movement.

> *Prophesy to the breath, prophesy, son of man, and say to the breath, thus says the Lord God: "Come from the four winds,* (the fourth dimension) *O breath, and breathe on these slain, that they may live." So, I prophesied as He commanded me, and breath came into them, and they lived, and stood upon their feet, an exceedingly great army* (Ezekiel 37:5–7).

To observe a cross section of an individual's solid surface in the four-dimensional world, we can divide or bisect a sliver of it to obtain a small sample of a person's history or a basic storyline. If we now take a cross section of that recorded timeline, we will obtain a single point or isolated event in that person's life history. The people we meet and the objects we see in our three-dimensional world are only a small fragment of what is available for us to know in the superior, inexhaustible fourth dimension of the boundless prophetic spirit world.

Prophetic words contain a powerful, creative light that initiates a spiritual movement (a realignment and coming together of a foundational structure) of bones, muscles, sinew and a new wineskin covering.

When I meet you in person with my physical senses, I am only seeing a page in one of the chapters of your Book of Life that revealed to me a small portion of who you really are in the realm of the Spirit. But if I can touch, feel and see you with my five higher spiritual senses, I can taste a sample of who you are in order to know and discern the vast potential found hidden deep within the real you. *By their fruits you will know them* (Matthew 7:20).

By discerning a person's past while clearly seeing their future, the choice words that are spoken will open amazing opportunities for them to access their greatest potential. Their fresh understanding of the ways of God moving in their imagination will renew their hopeful expectations for success.

Word of Knowledge

The word of knowledge can give me very specific insights into your past and present, while the discerning of spirits joined with the spirit of prophesy can reveal your untapped gifts and future potential. To know you by spirit, I must see and know the real, changeable you, the one who can adjust to the Word of God. We all fluctuate from conception (birth, life) to death, to resurrection from the dead into the fluidity of the coexisting realms of sensory impressions in the Spirit.

When we prophesy by the Ruach (the creative breath of God to that unanimated body), the breath of the Spirit enters in to resurrect a person, so he or she can hear the voice of God, recognize his or her concealed potential and see his or her divine purposes.

Our days are written in the books of heaven for the pure and shining one. Lord, you know everything there is to know about me, so investigate my heart (imagination) *as if it is an open book for You to get all the first hand facts about my life. You know my comings and goings. I am never out of Your sight. You perceive every movement of my heart and soul. You understand my every thought before it even enters my mind. You are so intimately aware of me, Lord.*

You read my heart like an open book. You know every word I am going to speak even before I have formulated the sentence in my head. You know my every step that I will take before my journey even begins. You surround me on all sides as a reassuring presence. You've gone into my future to prepare the way, and in kindness You follow behind me to spare me from the harm of my past. With Your hand of love upon my life, You impart a blessing to me that is so deep and wonderful that it is incomprehensible. The way You understand me strengthens my spirit and causes me to wonder.

There is no where I could go to hide from Your face or avoid Your omnipresence and all-seeing eyes! If I climb the mountain to touch the sky, you are there! If I ascend to heaven, You are there! If I go underground to the realms of the dead, You are there too! When I fly on the wings of the brilliant dawn morning, You are there waiting for me to arrive! Wherever I go, Your strong hand has guided me there. Your strength will empower me, the rising of Your shining helps me to navigate the darkness. It is impossible to disappear in the darkness from Your powerful presence of light. The darkness of night and the bright light of day are all the same to You.

My innermost being was formed by You. My delicate inside and my intricate outside were woven together by You in my mother's womb. Thank you for being so breathtakingly beautiful! You make me so mysteriously complex. Body and soul, I am marvelously made! I worship in adoration—what a creation! It simply amazes me to think about it! How thoroughly You know me, Lord! You know me inside and out, You know every bone in my body; You know exactly how I was made, bit by bit, how I was sculpted from nothing into something. You even formed every bone in my body when You created me in the secret place, carefully and skillfully shaping me from nothing, molding me into something.

Like an open book, You watched me grow from conception to birth; all the stages of my life were spread out before You. The days of my life were all prepared and determined for me before I'd even lived one day. Lord, You saw who You created me to be before I became me! Before I'd ever seen the light of day, the number of days You planned for me were already recorded in Your book for every single moment You are thinking of me! Your higher thoughts cherish me constantly. Your loving thoughts toward me are precious and beautiful; I could not begin to count them for they are as many as the sand of the sea. Your imaginations and desires toward me are wonderful! God, help me to comprehend them! When I sleep You imprint dreams and visions on my imagination. As I awake to arise each morning, You are there with me to interpret and show me my path.

God, come to slay the bloodthirsty, murderous people who blaspheme Your name, lifting themselves against Your purposes in vain. Cause the wicked to depart from me! I despise those who despise You. I grieve in disgust when they rise up to speak against You. I hate those who hate You with a pure, unadulterated hatred. Your godless arrogant enemies are my enemies!

God, come search, test and cross-examine my heart to reveal a clear picture of who IAM. IAM searching for who You have called me to become. Gaze in and examine me, sift through my anxious cares, see if IAM doing anything that is wrong. Investigate my whole life, find out everything about me past, present and future. Reveal what is hidden within me—then guide me on the road to eternal life. See if IAM walking on any path of pain. Lead me back to Your glorious, everlasting ways—onto the path that brings me back to my first love of You and Your eternal higher ways of life. Lord, be exalted through me (Psalm 139)*!*

Based on Psalm 139, through the word of knowledge, I am able to access your past and present timeline, to open any completed chapter in your Book of Life. I am able to know a cross section of your historical experiences, both glorious triumphs and devastating failures. As the Holy Spirit leads, I can read the section of your life's history that contains your present hopes and aspirations or current regrets. Through the Holy Spirit's gifts, I can also see, prophesy or decree things to alter and enhance the components of future probabilities that are waiting to be animated and obtained by you.

When we concentrate the power of our inner force (the Holy Spirit) on observing a certain thing as a priority, everything else will take second place or temporarily fade away. Letting go of the past and forgiving always makes room for a larger, better present existence. Living in a hopeful present attitude of expectation empowers our faith to draw the future into our now. When the Holy Spirit helps us to develop a higher self-concept (set new goals and aspire to rise above our current level of understanding), the transformation process has begun. This solid, three-dimensional world that we consider to be our reality is only an abstract shadow of the fourth dimension—the invisible, seemingly intangible realm of the Spirit.

When we prophesy by the Ruach (the creative breath of God to that unanimated body), the breath of the Spirit enters in to resurrect a person, so he or she can hear the voice of God, recognize his or her concealed potential and see his or her divine purposes.

In the realm of the Spirit, there's far more here than meets the eye. The earthly things we see are here today and gone tomorrow. But the invisible, spiritual things we don't often see but spiritually perceive now will last forever. *While we do not look at the things which are seen, but at the things which are not seen. For the things which are seen are temporary, but the things which are not seen are eternal* (2 Corinthians 4:18).

Responsibility and Accountability

Dream seers and interpreters become the redeeming liberators—the knights in shining armor who bring revolutionary answers and keys that unlock the mysteries contained within the heart. They rescue the fallen and deliver the abandoned, oppressed and distressed, because they always see into the future to observe and empower a person's potential, not his or her limitations. The world admires the dreamer who continually raises the bar higher and higher, setting a standard of excellence in every place of mediocrity. Those who fail to achieve their desires and goals in life fall short of their God-given potential and allocated measure of glory.

Prophets, seers, dreamers and apostolic visionaries are the builders of reality, the sculptors of a sustainable beauty, who inspire others to use their creative imaginations in their search for the seemingly invisible face of God. These spiritual leaders are given heavenly scrolls and strategic maps that reveal destiny to help us become wise master builders. The true measure of a godly leader is what he does with the power he is granted. Almost everyone can endure adversity, but a leader's character is tested when given the power to rule and reign. Power alone will reveal what's really hidden in a person's heart.

> *Prophets, seers, dreamers and apostolic visionaries are the builders of reality, the sculptors of a sustainable beauty, who inspire others to use their creative imaginations in their search for the face of the invisible God.*

When we dream and trust in God's process, we have entered into the double doors of favored access that no man can shut. These open doors of consciousness make the fulfillment of our lofty dreams inevitable. Whatever vision we cherish within our heart and place our continual desire and focus upon, we can be sure that we will eventually obtain it.

When the beauty of God's presence fills our mind, His pure and lovely thoughts will clothe us with His grace and empower us to dream and achieve our highest aspirations. God's perfect love casts out all fear. His love causes no pain or harm. Our dreams are the blueprints that show our creative imagination the divine strategies and plans that God has created for us to unravel the future. God's divine plans have been concealed within the threads of our own DNA. The visions we imagine are the spiritual images God is showing us of our promised destiny being fulfilled.

Prayer is the petition for wisdom, a plea for God's help to be granted, so that we can fulfill our destiny. Prophecy is our declaration of God's promise and help to establish what we believe, see, agree with and decree we will be.

In the natural realm of knowledge, we use the physical senses and properties of our mind to mentally define a person, a happening or an event. We use our natural eyes to look at and compare and contrast ourself to others. We analyze, reason, talk about and quail at the vast divergence we find in our current world of existence because it does not match what we desire to become. We contrast our present condition with the perceived success that we think is abounding in the lives of others. *For if you live according to the flesh you will die; but if you live by the Spirit you put to death the deeds of the body, then you will live* (Romans 8:13).

In order to function as spiritual beings led by the Spirit of God, we must discover that we can only truly know something by the Spirit. We can only know something by the Spirit if we are transformed into its image by taking on its likeness and actually accessing its power to become it. Every great achievement, creation or invention was at one time only a thought—a seedling of reality, a mere dream of hope being manifested in the mind of a Believer.

When we dream while resting in the realm of the Spirit, we discover how to die to the old and let go of our present concept of our natural, earthly self. When we perceive a God-given ideal, we cannot remain the same. When creative thoughts emerge within our imagination or the obscure realm of vision, they start the process of transformation.

Every great achievement, creation or invention was at one time only a thought, a seedling of reality, a mere dream of hope being manifested in the mind of a Believer.

Imagination travels outside of our concrete physical boundaries. Spiritual knowledge vastly outweighs natural knowledge. Spiritual knowledge has an eternal weight of value that creates eternal change within our being. No one is able to evolve into a higher state of being by natural means or by simply wishing it to be so. Every thought, whether positive or negative, will create a condition that will produce an adjoining effect or reaction.

In order to change, it is essential that we be transformed by the spiritual renewing of our mind. We do this by taking on the mind of Christ. The mind of Christ causes us to be consciously aware of His higher power living, breathing and moving within us. Cooperating with God's infinite power and wisdom empowers us to govern the breadths of our inner-gifted, spiritual fourth dimensions in order to alter, rule and reign the expansive outer physical world.

We will become as great as our highest imagined aspiration or fall as low as our strongest ruling weakness. *The Book of the Law shall not depart from your mouth, but we are to read, meditate* (or imagine) *on it day and night* (Joshua 1:8). When we minister to the lowest levels of humanity as if they are equal to the highest, we create a platform of honor. This platform opens a conscious door of opportunity for everyone to advance and ascend out of the pit of depravation. People are able to evolve by taking on a new image and Christlike identity. When we show honor to people, we make it possible for them to choose to emerge differently, to obtain a new identity that will empower them to evolve and reach their highest potential.

> *We will become as great as our highest imagined aspiration or fall as low as our strongest ruling weakness.*

Don't fawn over certain influential people in an attempt to find favor with them in order to advance. Learn to treat everyone equally. Show no partiality, prejudice, snobbery or preference. Say you encounter a rich man who is wearing designer clothes and his hands are adorned with gold and diamond rings. Would you treat him differently than a poor man in shabby clothes? Would you pay special attention to the wealthy man? Would you offer him the preferable seat, while you ignore the poor man and say, "You can stand over there," or "Sit on the floor at my feet!" Are you not discriminating among your own, being critic and judge with selfish and wrong motives? God has chosen the poor in the eyes of the world to be rich in faith as Believers. To those who love Him, God has promised that they will inherit the Kingdom (see James 2:1–5).

Every one of us should reach up to trace our fingertips across the brail bumps that form the new name we have been given in Christ. Each one of us has been given a different way to manifest one of God's names. The IAM has been imprinted as a seal upon our foreheads to prepare us for this new season of strength, powerful influence and authority. *They shall see His face, and His name shall be on their foreheads* (Revelation 22:4). Believers have been sealed with the finger of God's Holy Spirit.

Jesus names each one of us based on our future potential, not on our past mistakes. He anoints our head with oil so that we can know who we are in Christ. Once we know who we are in Christ, we can gain an understanding of where we are going. God is giving each of us a NEW NAME that is written on a white stone. The Holy Spirit has expanded our IDENTITY in Him so that our Christ-centered identity will reflect our new strength based in the might of Christ's Spirit—His Christlike identity, power and kingdom authority.

> *Therefore repent; or else I AM coming to you quickly, and I will make war against them with the sword of My mouth. He, who has an ear, let him hear what the Spirit says to the churches. To him who overcomes, to him I will give some of the hidden manna, and I will give him a white stone, and a new name written on the stone which no one knows but he who receives it* (Revelation 2:16–17).

A new identity means that we also need new, broader connections with new ways of doing things! The nations shall see your righteousness and vindication, your rightness and justice, not your own but His ascribed to you. All kings shall behold your salvation and glory, and you shall be called by a new name, which the mouth of the Lord shall name. You shall also be so beautiful and prosperous, to be thought of as a crown of glory and honor in the hand of the Lord, a royal diadem exceedingly beautiful in the hand of your God (see Isaiah 62).

Every single one of us is a continual work still in progress. Each one of us is being added to, and we are all at a different maturity and on diverse gifting levels. We are becoming new creatures in Christ. *God will make you complete in every good work to do His will, working in you what is well pleasing in His sight, through Jesus Christ, to whom be glory forever and ever* (Hebrews 13:21).

When we take ourself off the king's throne, we yield another area of our life to God's sovereign rule.

> *He who sits on the throne said, "Behold, I am making All Things new." And He said, "Write, for these words are faithful and true." Then He said to me, "It is done. I am the Alpha and the Omega, the Beginning and the End. I will give to the one who thirsts from the spring of the water of life without cost. He who overcomes will inherit these things, and I will be his God and he will be My son"* (Revelation 21:5–7).

By trading in all that we are to become all that God has designed for us to be, only then can we become like all of Him.

Let Us Pray

Dear Holy Spirit, teach us to hear the leading of Your gentle voice whispering in our ears. Let us feel the pleasant movements of Your motions as You stir up our spirits to prophesy according to the command of the breath of the Spirit. Help us transcend the natural realms of reasoning and enter into the unlimited measure of the Spirit found in the fourth dimension. Fill our mouths with the words that release the life-giving resurrection power to those who have been slain by the disappointments of life. Let the weight of Your higher truth resonate within our hearts. Shake us out of complacency, and bring us together in the unity of one spirit. Let the powerful wind of Your Spirit breathe life into those who were slain so that they stand up as an exceedingly great army. Amen.

CHAPTER ELEVEN

Heavenly Prayer Portal

All of the world's prayers converge in Israel. Although Israel has a physically small geographic circumference, it is the largest spiritually active prayer portal in the entire world. Every single one of the prayers that people (from all over the earth) offer to God travel to Israel through an intricate network of invisible spiritual gateways.

These strategic labyrinths are opened and closed by angels who are used to funnel prayers through these heavenly channels and spiritual switch systems all the way to Israel. All of the prayers that are offered by every tribe, tongue and nation, even in different geographic areas around the world, travel through these angelic gateways. The prayers of the whole world are all gathered together from each individual person and endless prayer network. These prayers converge in Israel to be woven into one massively powerful, flaming tornado of intertwined energy threads consisting of vibrantly multicolored, braided light rods. They are all joined and knit together before they ascend up to heaven in a massive, roaring, fiery portal of power.

Our prayers all converge and unite as one enormous pillar of blazing fire before they are released to exit the earth's atmosphere. Our prayers arise as an intense, furious tower of power that transcends space to ascend and enter into heaven's throne room. Once the prayers of God's people enter heaven, they are weighed, measured and savored. The prayers release an aroma, a fragrance that is smelled, and they are sorted and poured out into different bowls.

Angels then offer these full prayer bowls to God as fiery coals of fragrant incense upon His heavenly altar. God enjoys smelling their sweet aromatic incenses. He weighs and judges the faith contained in every prayer, and He determines the amount of revelation knowledge each person can receive. At the fullness of time, God retrieves and releases the specific reply that is needed to answer our prayer request. God knows and keeps all of the varied answers to our prayerful questions that have been waiting for us to ask.

There are treasuries that are chock-full of God's vast wisdom, endless solutions and detailed answers to prayer. They have all been residing there in heaven, lingering in the Spirit, eagerly waiting for us to access them. Wisdom has been waiting from before the foundation of the world, anticipating the time when we would finally call upon her.

Once the answer is chosen, the correct angelic messengers are summoned and quickly dispatched. Angels awaken our imagination to show us the answers to our prayers. They are skilled at helping us interpret the dreams and visions that are called up from deep within our being. Angels show us the higher ways to go. They come to escort us to heaven when it is time for us to go home, and they ascend and descend up heavenly ladders to celebrate the spiritual birth of every new Believer.

Our prayers arise as an intense, furious tower of power that transcends space to ascend and enter into heaven's throne room.

Salvation cannot be inherited simply by being born to Christian parents or by attending or joining a church, mosque or synagogue. Salvation does not come by having a residence located somewhere in America. Salvation comes to each individual person, and it must be accepted and worked out or denied on a one-on-one basis. The regenerated man of the flesh as the firstborn natural son has been led and dominated by the earthly sensual expressions throughout his life. *The first man was of the earth, made of dust; the second Man is the Lord from heaven* (1 Corinthians 15:47).

After our spirit experiences a rebirth, we enter into salvation. *Then the first earthly man must become last and the last spirit man shall become the first* (Matthew 19:30).

People led by their spirit learn how to submit their soul to the leading of their spirit. *So that He it is, who's coming after me is preferred before me* (John 1:27). Spiritual conversion is a supernatural transformation of one's identity that empowers him or her to apprehend his or her extraordinary future. This divine makeover is a spiritual overhaul that pulls us up Jacob's Ladder and into another grand reality. When we are in Christ, we are given the wisdom that is needed to successfully navigate any perceived challenge or impossibilities that are found in the invisible realms of faith.

Heavenly Ladders and God's Messengers

The Bible records a ladder of ascending and descending angelic presence that rested upon both Nathaniel and Jacob (refer to Volume II for a refresher on Jacob's Ladder and spiritual gateways). These two earthly witnesses felt, saw and experienced an open heaven and communicated with angels. That same revelatory ladder rests upon each one of us too! If we train our imagination to sense and feel the invisible spiritual realms, we will have angels on heavenly ladders ascending and descending upon us.

Believers in Christ Jesus become the ladders that angels journey back and forth on. Angels come down this ladder from the Father of Light to touch people, impart anointings and deliver messages and divine giftings. Even the Godhead had their own archangel assigned to them. The Archangel Michael (means *who is like God*) served God the Father as a warrior angel for Israel, the apple of His eye. The Archangel Gabriel (means *strong man of God*) is the messenger angel who serves the Holy Spirit. And lucifer (means *light bringer* or *bearer*) once served Jesus as the morning star, the son of dawn, the cherub of worship and praise.

If we train our imagination to sense and feel the invisible spiritual realms, we will have angels on heavenly ladders ascending and descending upon us.

When angels have completed their assignment, they do not hang around to chat with people. These majestic beings descend back up the spiral (helix) ladder into heaven to report their findings. Then they receive a new message, designation or commission before they return to earth again. Believers are earthen vessels that become spiritual gateways. We connect with the angelic realms and the powerful light of God's heavenly revelation; our lives give it entrance into earth.

Once Nathaniel accessed Jesus (the door) as his Savior, he was given a vision of a heavenly ladder. When Nathaniel was conscious of Jesus as His Savior and the reality of a heavenly ladder, he understood how to ascend into the higher heights to gain the spiritual understanding that had been there waiting for him his whole life. When we receive salvation, we can access this same revelation and experience too!

New heavenly structures, alignments and forms bring forth a fresh vision, new opportunities and an expanded expression of our being. Dreams design divine strategies that deliver answers to our challenges. Godly wisdom grants us bold authority, revelation knowledge and imaginative, creative power that produce an unlimited stream of possibilities for our destinies. To the degree that we are willing to submit, study, learn, and change, we can continually enhance our destiny.

Godly wisdom grants us bold authority, revelation knowledge and imaginative, creative power that produce an unlimited stream of possibilities for our destinies.

The Holy Spirit in us always encompasses and gently surrounds us while He reveals expanded levels or states of revelation knowledge. The hidden realms of the Spirit are deep within the Christ who resides in us. To access these deeper realms of revelation, we must access more of the love of Christ. Father God reveals revelation knowledge to His Son, Jesus, who, in turn, tells the Holy Spirit. Holy Spirit then shares His secrets with us, His beloved children, friends, saints and Bride.

Intimacy with God transforms us until we become an integral part of the eternal circle of God's revelation knowledge. We are the earthly change agents and spiritual conduits that bring the Kingdom of God to manifestation on earth. The Holy Spirit relates to us according to our spiritual identity in Christ, not according to our own self-image, personal belief system or our (Esau) earthly behavior.

Let Us Pray

Jesus, You are the eternal door to heaven. Jesus Christ, You are righteous, the glorious advocate with the Father who makes intercession for me. Every day, I hear Your words speak Your messages of love to me, for You command Your lovingkindness toward me. At night, You sing comforting songs over me. I hear Your continual prayers for me, and they have become my life. Your tender voice of love whispers Your knowledge to our hearts (see Psalms 19:2; 42:8). Teach me to pray as You pray. Awaken me to see, feel and acknowledge the angels that do Your bidding. Transform me into Your image and likeness so that I can commune with You in intimacy as an integral part of the eternal circle. Amen.

CHAPTER TWELVE

Brenda Doreen Breathitt

At times, Jesus Himself arises from His heavenly throne to bring us the answer to our prayers in a visitation.

I was awake praying late into the night on September 7, 2019. My dear, sweet baby sister, Brenda, lay terminally ill in Lakeland, Florida, where she had been battling kidney cancer for many months. She had stopped eating but was still holding onto life, just waiting for me, Mom and my brother, Steven, to come visit her one last time.

As I lie awake in Texas, praying in the darkest hours of the early morning, I asked the Holy Spirit, "May I, please, talk to Brenda's spirit to tell her how much I love her, how proud I am of her and to say goodbye?"

I wanted Brenda to know how much she meant to me both as a sister and lifelong best friend. Although I really desired to be there with Brenda physically to help her transition to heaven, I knew I could still touch and comfort her in the Spirit through prayer. Brenda knew we were not coming back to see her again, so I sought to be with Brenda so that she would not be alone.

"Brenda, even though I cannot be there with you in the body of the flesh, because we are separated geographically, my spirit is present there with you. I'm happy to see how disciplined and deeply committed you are in your faith in Christ, the Anointed One" (see Colossians 2:5).

I wanted to hold my sweet Brenda as she let go of the last ounces of life that lingered within her. She was so strong. She had fought a great, courageous fight, holding onto life so that she could be with the family and friends she loved so much. God knew that I wanted to be with Brenda when she finally transitioned peacefully into heaven.

The Holy Spirit granted my prayerful request to share my heartfelt love with Brenda. I asked her if she had seen Jesus yet. She replied, "No, but I have seen Dad several times! I have seen Dad's radiant face. He has come to me, full of light, shining brightly at the end of a dark tunnel. He is showing me the way to go."

At times, Jesus Himself arises from His heavenly throne to bring us the answer to our prayers in a visitation.

As I finished sharing my heartfelt love with Brenda, I suddenly saw a brilliant light as Jesus appeared in her family room. Jesus walked up to Brenda's hospice bed. He took her beautiful, needle-bruised hands in His beautiful, nail-scared hands to gently kiss them. I watched as Brenda's countenance lit up with joyful excitement. She was so thrilled to see her Jesus standing right in front of her. Brenda had never seen Jesus before. Then Jesus said to her:

> "I love you so much, Brenda! I have come to ask which way you want Me to pour the prayer bowls. I will follow the decision you want to make." Jesus went on to tell her, "Barbie has mobilized the whole world to pray for your healing and deliverance from cancer. When Barbie reluctantly left your bedside to go to Hong Kong and Malaysia for those ten days, I promised her that if she did that trip for My Kingdom, I would do something special for her.
>
> Barbie mobilized the Asian people to pray day and night for your miracle. Malaysia already had a miracle gate open, but while Barbie was there ministering, I granted an answer to her prayers for an upgrade when she decreed for Malaysia's Miracle Gate to become a Creative Miracle Gateway into the world. Barbie has requested a creative miracle that would restore your body back to its perfected state. She wants you to join her in a miracle ministry that will impact

> the world from Glory of Zion Global Spheres Ministries in Corinth, Texas.
>
> Brenda, I have come to tell you that people's prayers from all around the world have filled the prayer bowls in heaven on your behalf. The testimony of your body being completely restored to wholeness from a creative miracle, from the ravages of cancer that has devoured your skeletal structure, will ignite hope in people all over the world. Now I need to know which way you want Me to pour the bowls? I can grant you the creative miracle that will completely restore your earthly body so that you can fulfill your destiny here on earth as a miracle worker. Or I can give you your spiritual body, and you can come to heaven with Me right now."

Having seen Jesus' beauty and having felt the tender, loving touch of His marred hands, Brenda made the only choice possible. Above all the fame and fortune brought forth by the realms of creative miracles and healing ministry, with its accolades for supernatural gifts hosted in people, Brenda chose to depart this earthly life to be with her beloved Jesus. The words of the Bible tell us that, "Precious are His loving ones in the sight of the Lord; the death of His saints is very important to Him."

Brenda Doreen Breathitt passed into eternity with her Jesus on Saturday, September 7, 2019, at 4:00 a.m.

That Sunday, Mom and I sat in the worship service at Glory of Zion in Corinth, Texas. During the service of September 8, every word of knowledge that was given for healing dealt with all of the conditions from which Brenda needed to be healed. The minister called out kidney cancer, bone cancer that caused the deterioration of the backbone, a broken femur and crushed hip bones. It was as if Brenda was up in heaven executing vengeance on all of the symptoms (excruciating pain and great suffering) the cancer had caused her to endure for so many months.

Brenda left her beautiful daughter, Chelsea Cribb, and her husband, Clif, behind—along with me, her mom, Nan, her favorite brother, Steven, my sister, Lin, and her husband, Virgil. But she gained Jesus, the lover of her soul, her father, Douglas, her grandmother, Kate, Uncle Harvie, Aunt Ann,

Granny, Gramps, her dog, Lady, and all others who had gone on before her.

During her fifty-two years of life, Brenda was a very loving, caring and selfless person. She lived her life in service to others, listening to their woes and taking care of their needs. Yet you never heard Brenda complain. She was always positive and cheerful, even in the hospital with broken, deteriorating, cancer-ridden bones. She brightened up a room with her big, beautiful smile and contagious, bold laughter. So in death, she did the same.

When she weighed the results of her receiving a brand new physical body or laying down her life as a sacrificial seed for her friends around the world to receive creative miracles on a mass scale, she chose to sow herself as a spiritual seed that would bring forth multiplied testimonies of creative miracle fruits. No greater love has anyone than this: that she lay down her own life for her friends. Brenda was a seed that fell into the ground and died so that others could receive their creative miracle here on earth.

That Sunday morning, Dr. Chuck Pierce confirmed from Glory of Zion's stage that the Lord told him that Brenda was a seed to bring forth creative miracles throughout the world.

> *I assure you, most solemnly I tell you, unless a kernel of wheat falls into the ground and dies, it remains only a single seed, it never becomes more but lives by itself alone. But if it dies, it produces many other seeds and yields a rich harvest. Anyone who loves their life will lose it, while anyone who hates their life in this world will keep it for eternal life. Whoever has no love for, no concern for, no regard for her life here on earth, but despises it, preserves her life forever and ever. Whoever serves Me must continue to follow Me conform wholly to My example in living, and if need be, in dying; and where I am, My servant also will be. My Father will honor the one who serves Me* (John 12:24–26).

God chose each one of us to dwell in Him from before the foundation of the world, that we should be holy and without blame before Him in love (Ephesians 1:4).

The God that we serve is not a respecter of persons, so I pray:

> *The God of our Lord Jesus Christ, the Father of glory, may give to you a spirit of wisdom and of revelation in the knowledge of Him. I pray that the eyes of your heart may be enlightened, so that you will know what is the hope of His calling, what are the riches of the glory of His inheritance in the saints, and what is the surpassing greatness of His power toward us who believe* (Ephesians 1:17–19).

My dear friend Dr. Margilee Hylton told me of a vision she had of my late sister on October 2, 2019, shortly after Brenda had passed into glory. Margilee said:

> "I never personally met Brenda, but I prayed for her during her battle with kidney cancer. I dreamt Brenda was on a rope climbing up this high mountain. She was clothed in a garment of light with such brilliance. I have not the capacity to measure or explain in mere words the realm of glory I saw. Brenda was trying to tell me something to relay to you but the words were not words as we know them. There was just light in the form of clouds coming from her mouth. Brenda was consumed by and surrounded with the light of God. Her eyes had the same gleam like yours. However, the gleam in her eyes was saturated with this brilliant light! Finally, I saw Brenda adorning you in a tunic-like, teal garment made out of indescribably beautiful, pure silk. Brenda was radiating with a brilliant light. I will never forget the splendor and beauty of the heavenly realm of glory that she was in."

In the realm of the Spirit, the color of teal represents the following: taking the initiative for an emotional healing; a calm serenity of self-awareness and creative expressions; being led by your heartfelt feelings instead of rational thinking. Teal means that you have a rich sophistication and expensive elegance about you. As a friend, teal means the following: you are protective of others; stable; constant and consistent; trustworthy; reliable; your strength is a sensitivity that promotes spiritual advancement; you are devoted to friends and family; you are optimistic and trusting of others with a high degree of faith and hope. The color teal indicates that you have a loyal, devoted nature that is willing to help those who need physical, emotional or spiritual assistance.

Margilee's vision of Brenda was a real encouragement to me in a time of grief, as Brenda had been my best friend in the world.

Let Us Pray

Dear heavenly Father, please help me to be willing to be like the kernel of wheat that falls to the ground and dies. I do not want to enter into eternity alone without any fruit to show for my life. Help me to die to my own self desires and personal agendas. I want to be a person of grace who produces many seeds and yields a rich harvest of souls for Your Kingdom. Help me not to love my life, but let me lose it on earth, while preserving it in eternity by serving others. Amen.

CHAPTER THIRTEEN

Hindrances to Prayer

Doubt is the strongest hindrance to receiving an answer to prayer. We must ask in faith with no wavering, no hesitating and no doubting. The person who wavers also hesitates and doubts. He is like a billowing surge out at sea that is continually blown here and there, tossed by every wind and wave. This type of person should not imagine that he will receive anything he asks for from the Lord in prayer. This man has two different minds that hesitate, and he is procrastinating, vague and vacillating. Therefore, he is unstable, unreliable and always uncertain about everything he thinks, feels and decides (see James 1:6–8).

To get prayers for healing answered, we must be a man or woman of faith who is careful about what he or she thinks or imagines, and we must believe God's Word without doubting. To begin a prayer with a statement like, "God, if it be Your will to heal," is to pray in doubt and unbelief. It demonstrates a lack of faith in God's miracle-working power, no understanding of God's will and a lack of knowledge of the written Word.

Being in full-time ministry, I have prayed many faith-filled prayers, laid hands on the sick to see them recover and seen many miracles instantly take place. But I have also seen, heard and witnessed people's doubt-filled prayers, bad council and ignorant advice, which tore down others' expectant faith for a miracle, and those being prayed for did not receive any healing results. So many well-meaning but ignorant people focus on the facts of someone's diagnosis or disease, reciting what a doctor has stated rather than in faith believing what the Word of God says is true.

The Bible clearly indicates that when we have rejected the knowledge of God, we are destroyed for a lack of knowledge (see Hosea 4:6). Scripture further states in many passages that healing *is* the will of God, for it is the children's bread. Jesus took forty brutal stripes that ripped open and shredded the flesh on His bare back for our healing. Jesus shed His precious blood for our healing. *When you speak healing words, you offer others fruit from the Tree of Life. But unhealthy, negative words do nothing but crush their hopes* (Proverbs 15:4).

> *To get prayers for healing answered, we must be a man or woman of faith who is careful about what he or she thinks or imagines, and we must believe God's Word without doubting.*

Nothing is more appealing than speaking beautiful, life-giving words. For they release sweetness to our souls and inner healing to our spirits (Proverbs 16:24).

Do you know someone who is always besieged with one sickness, infirmity or disease after another? Chances are they have experienced too much rejection, disappointment, disillusionment and regret. Pray for that person's broken heart to be healed and for his or her joy to be restored so that he or she will finally win the battle. *A joyful, cheerful heart brings healing to both body and soul. But the one whose heart is crushed struggles with sickness and depression* (Proverbs 17:22).

Prayer must contain specific information and declarations and decrees of Scripture that describe your request. The angelic realms will not take action until the Word of God that is directed to a specific end is released with faith.

> *A great crowd formed as Jesus and His disciples were leaving Jericho. When Bartimaeus, a blind beggar, who was sitting by the roadside heard that it was Jesus of Nazareth, who was passing by he began to shout, saying, "Jesus, Son of David, have pity and mercy on me now!" The crowd severely rebuked and censured him with their reproof shouting for him to hold his peace and keep still, but Bartimaeus shouted all the more,*

> *"Son of David, have pity on me!" Jesus stopped and called to him. Throwing off his beggar's garment* (a physical statement of faith that he would no longer make his living as a beggar), *Bartimaeus leaped up and ran to Jesus. And Jesus asked him to be specific in his request, "Bartimaeus exactly what do you want Me to do for you?" And the blind man replied to Jesus, "Master, let me receive my sight"* (Mark 10:46 51).

The art of prayer is exact and specific. You get what you believe and ask for in faith. If you believe that healing is not for today, for you healing is an impossibility that never happens. If we lack the love of Christ working in and through our life, our prayer life will be hindered. *For if we are in Christ Jesus, neither circumcision nor uncircumcision counts for anything, but only faith activated, energized, expressed and working through love* (Galatians 5:6).

> Jesus took forty stripes on His back and shed His precious blood for our healing.

Lay aside every weight of sin. Repent and let it go. Do not allow small things to hinder you. Worry is a hindrance. *Do not fret or have any anxiety about anything, but in every circumstance and in everything, by prayer, definite requests and petition with thanksgiving, continue to make your wants known to God* (Philippians 4:6). Stop worrying and give your petition to God by prayer. The Lion of the Tribe of Judah has prevailed for you. Look to see positive pictures and manifest them by praying in the Holy Spirit. The opposite of worry is the prayer of faith.

> *And who of you by worrying and being anxious can add one inch his stature or a day to the span of his life? And why should you be anxious about clothes? Consider the lilies of the field and learn thoroughly how they grow; they neither toil nor spin. Yet I tell you, even Solomon in all his magnificence excellence, dignity, and grace was not arrayed like one of these. But if God so clothes the grass of the field, which today is alive and green and tomorrow is tossed into the furnace, will He not much more surely clothe you, O you of little faith? Therefore, do not worry and be anxious, saying, "What are we going to have to eat?" or, "What are we going to have to drink?" or "What*

> *are we going to have to wear?" For the heathen Gentiles wish for and crave and diligently seek all these things, and your heavenly Father knows well that you need them all* (Matthew 6:27–32).

Elijah Confronts the False Prophets

God groups us according to how we think and imagine. The Prophet Elijah had problems with his thinking. He suffered from depression, self-pity and isolationism because he thought he was the only prophet who was left to serve God. Elijah was taken up to heaven in a whirlwind. Elijah's servant, Elisha, replaced him and did twice the miracles of Elijah during his time of ministry.

> *The spiritual man walks with God by exercising the creative faith of God.*

> *After Elijah appeared before King Ahab in the barren wilderness, he requested Ahab send all the inhabitants of Israel and assembled the false prophets at Mount Carmel. Elijah came near to the nation of people asking, "How long will you tarry between two opinions?" But they were silent answering not a word. Most people are followers, so they do not have opinions. They are not leaders, so they quietly stand watching on the sidelines saying and doing nothing. When someone is complacent, standing idly by as a spectator, nothing of substance ever happens for them.*

> *Elijah announced, "I am only one prophet yet IAM challenging 450 false prophets of Baal who serve this unjust corrupt government. If the Lord is God, follow Him! But if Baal is your god, then follow him. Let two bulls be given us; let them choose one bull for themselves and cut it in pieces and lay it on the wood but put no fire to it. I will dress the second bull, lay it on the wood, and put no fire to it. Then you call on the name of your god, and I will call on the name of the Lord; and the One God who answers by fire, let Him be God." And all the people answered, "It is well spoken."'*

Hundreds of false prophets called on the name of Baal, leaping and limping around the altar from morning until noon, begging, "O Baal, hear and answer us!" But there was no voice; no one answered. Elijah mocked them at noon, "If Baal is a god he is daydreaming or contemplating, gone astray, taken a vacation or perhaps he is asleep and you must cry out louder, and cut yourselves with knives until your blood gushes to awaken him." Midday passed, and they were weary as they played the part of prophets until the time for offering the evening sacrifice, but there was still no voice, no answer and no one who paid attention.

Then the Prophet Elijah gathered all the people near. In preparation for a visitation from God, Elijah repaired the old altar of the Lord that Jezebel had destroyed. Elijah took twelve stones to represent God's government for each of the Twelve Tribes of the sons of Jacob, whom the Lord gave the name Israel. He dug a deep trench that could hold two measures of seed around the altar as a symbol of separation from the world. He dug up, removed and cut off all the roots in the ditch.

Elijah laid the wood (represents the cross) *in order. He cut the bull in pieces* (represents the great cost of the shed blood of the sacrifice) *and placed it on top of the pier. He commanded, "Fill four large jars with water and pour it on the burnt offering and the wood." And he said, "Do it the second time* (4 x 2 = 8; represents the resurrection power of a new beginning; eight has no beginning or end—it continues to loop like eternity). *And they did it the second time. And he said, "Do it the third time." And they did it the third time making a total of twelve* (3 x 4 = 12; represents God's government) *pitchers of water being poured out and sacrificed in the time of drought. The costly water* (represents the Word and Spirit of God) *ran over and saturated the altar. Elijah filled the trench around about with water.*

At the time of the offering of the evening sacrifice, Elijah the prophet came near with a great expectation of seeing the power of God demonstrated. He spoke to the Lord, the God of Abraham, Isaac and Israel, saying, "Let it be known this day that You are the only true God in Israel and that I am Your servant and that I have done all these things at Your Word. Now Hear me, O Lord, that this people may know that You, the Lord, are the only God, and have turned their hearts back to You."

Then the fire of the Lord fell from heaven. God's fire consumed the burnt sacrifice, the wood and the stones and the dust. The fire of God also licked up the water that had soaked the trench. When all the people saw it, they fell on their faces in worship to proclaim, "The Lord, He is God! The Lord, He is God!" Then Elijah told all of Israel to, "Seize the prophets of Baal; do not let one escape." They seized the false prophets, and Elijah brought them down to the brook Kishon, and slew them there as God's law required (1 Kings 18:20–40).

The Prophet Elijah exercised his spiritual senses to hear the sound of an abundance of rain coming from a cloud the size of a man's hand. Elijah heard a rainstorm coming out of a minute cloud during a time of drought, when the skies had been shut up for years. He declared, "I hear a profuse wealth of rain" (see 1 Kings 18:41–44)!

Our five natural senses still exist but are mirrored by our spiritual senses that are quickened or made alive to the Spirit of God when we are reckoned dead to the flesh. The spiritual man walks with God by exercising the creative faith of God. The external does not affect the Believer. Jesus said, "IAM in the world, but IAM not of the world." As a Believer, IAM not under the world's control. I do not react as the world reacts. God's ways are beyond the world's ability of finding out.

> When faith is on the throne of our heart, we perceive, hear, see and know things in and by the Spirit of God.

Believers are spiritually fed and led by the pneuma breath of life from God, the Fruit of the Spirit in Galatians 5 and the Gifts of the Spirit in 1 Corinthians 12. But the Sons of God move in the fullness of the seven different dimensions of the Holy Spirit's ministry of God in Isaiah 11:2, and they have continual access to the Revelation 4:1–2 open door to heaven.

> *The just shall live by faith. Now faith is the substance of things hoped for, the evidence of things not seen. For by it the elders obtained a good testimony. By faith we understand that the worlds were framed by the Word of God, so that the things which are seen were not made of things which are visible* (Hebrews 11:2–3).

Let Us Pray

Dear Jesus, I thank You that You died for my sins. You hung upon a cruel cross, and you shed Your life's blood so that I can be healed. You bore forty stripes upon Your back so that I can overcome sickness and all of the forty major diseases known to man. Help me receive a greater measure of faith, and baptize me in Your love. Deliver me from all sin, worry, doubt and unbelief. Deliver me from depression, self-pity and isolationism. Help me to serve You in the world but not to partake of any part of the world's ways. Amen.

CHAPTER FOURTEEN

The Mystery of Melchizedek

When faith is on the throne of our heart, we perceive, hear, see and know things in and by the Spirit of God. Believers have two sets of senses that feel, smell, taste, eyes that see and ears that hear. One is normal or natural. The other is divinely supernatural; it is part of our spiritual senses. Hear this now, O foolish people, without understanding, who have eyes and see not, and who have ears and hear not (Jeremiah 5:21). Spiritual people have a supernatural ability to hear what the Spirit is saying to individuals, the Church and world governments.

We will enter into the Melchizedekian priesthood having slain all of our unlovely thoughts, attitudes and the kings that rule from the thrones of negative ideas. We take on and reflect the image that we come to behold and rest in. When you decide to arise and shine, your brilliant light will draw kings and people of authority into your circle of influence.

Psalm 89:27 states of Jesus: *I will also make Him My firstborn preeminent, the highest of the kings of the earth.*

Who is He then, this King of Glory? The Lord of Hosts, He is the King of Glory who rules over all creation with His heavenly armies. Selah (Psalm 24:10).

Jesus is designated by God as the High Priest according to the order of Melchizedek (see Hebrews 5:10). And this becomes even more evident if another priest arises in the likeness of Melchizedek (see Hebrews 7:15).

As He also says in another place, "You are a priest appointed forever according to the order of Melchizedek" (Hebrews 5:6). It is beyond dispute that the lesser person is always blessed by the greater one (see Hebrews 7:7).

In Genesis, we read about Melchizedek, which means king of righteousness. Because he lived and ruled in the city of Salem, which means peace, Melchizedek was also known as the King of Peace. Melchizedek was the symbol of all that is good. He was the IAM, the priest of the Most High God. Melchizedek went out and met Abraham as Father Abraham returned from defeating many kings (adverse, harmful, destructive ideas) in battle, including King Chedorlaomer and his allies. Genesis 14:1 lists the names of four kings: Amraphel of Shinar; Aricoch of Ellasar; Chedorlaomer of Elam; Tidal of the Goiim.

> When you decide to arise and shine, your brilliant light will draw kings and people of authority into your circle of influence.

King Chedorlaomer met his demise after warring against the cities of the plain (Sodom, Gomorrah, Admah, Zebolim and Zoar) at the Valley of Siddim. King Chedorlaomer went down to Sodom and Gomorrah to collect booty and other spoils of war. He took Lot and his entire household captive. When Abram learned of Lot's predicament, he assembled a battle unit of three hundred eighteen men to pursue the Elamite forces north of Damascus to Hobah. One of the units of warriors led by Abram defeated and slaughtered Chedorlaomer and his men (see Genesis 14:11–17). *For the lips of the priest should guard and preserve knowledge of My law, and the people should seek instruction from his mouth; for he is the messenger of the Lord of hosts* (Malachi 2:7).

> *Then I saw a new heaven and a new earth, for the first heaven and the first earth had passed away vanished, and there is no longer any sea. And I saw the holy city, new Jerusalem, coming down out of heaven from God, arrayed like a Bride adorned for her husband; and then I heard a loud voice from the throne, saying, "See! The Tabernacle of God is among them, and they will be His people, and God Himself will be with them as their God, and He will wipe away every tear from their eyes; and there will no longer be sorrow and anguish, or crying, or*

> *pain, for the former order of things has passed away. Behold, IAM making All Things new! My words are faithful, accurate, incorruptible and true. You can place your trust in them. It is done! IAM the Alpha and Omega, the Beginning and the End. To the one who thirsts I will give the water of life without cost. Those who overcome the world by adhering to the faith of Christ Jesus as their Savior will inherit these things. I will be their God and they will be My Sons and Bride"* (Revelation 21:1–7).

You have made them to be a kingdom of royal subjects and priests to our God; and they will reign on the earth (Revelation 5:10).

When we are able to defeat the angry enemy kings that rule in our mind, heart and things that are around us, Melchizedek (Priest of the Most High God) will also bless us. Melchizedek blessed our ancestor. Although Melchizedek was not Jewish or a relative of Abraham, Abraham (the most honored and favored patriarch of God's chosen ones) gave Melchizedek a tenth (a tithe) of everything he had won from the spoils captured in battle. Showing gratitude and being thankful for individual battles that we win becomes a vital part of overcoming the evil kings, thoughts, attitudes and controlling kingdoms that try to rule over us.

> *Jesus is designated by God as the High Priest according to the order of Melchizedek.*

Scripture does not name Melchizedek's mother or father or his ancestors or descendants. He was never born, so his birth is not recorded in the Bible. Melchizedek will never die, so his death is never mentioned.

Jewish priests were the descendants of Levi, who were given the Law of Moses, so they could collect one tenth (a tithe) of the incomes from their relatives in the Twelve Tribes of Israel. Being mortal, they all died. But Melchizedek did not belong to the Tribe of Levi or any of the other tribes. Melchizedek lives on for eternity!

Melchizedek, being greater and superior than the mighty Abraham (Father of Faith), imparted a blessing on Abraham. *And Melchizedek blessed Abram and said, "Blessed joyful, favored be Abram by God Most High, Creator and*

Possessor of heaven and earth" (Genesis 14:19). Although Abraham had received the promises, it was Melchizedek who blessed Abraham. This made it possible for Abraham to increase vision and multiply understanding in order for him to build a structure to possess the promises.

The name Abraham means *exalted father*. He represents obedience and faith because he was tested again and again until he developed his strong faith in God. Abraham was willing to sacrifice his beloved son, Isaac, on the mountain of the Lord. He was willing to give up his most prized possession to obtain the Lord. The ram represents the residence and opposition of personality to the complete truth that must be sacrificed.

The greater always blesses the lesser. The wisdom found in the Father's blessing gives us an increased measure of favor and vision. Hope enables us to create the joy and sustain the patience that is necessary to possess the promise. At that time, Levi was still unborn (being in the loins of Abraham's mind, *dionaoa*, imagination; the region of the abdomen that houses the reproductive organs), yet he, too, paid an original tithe to Melchizedek. If the priesthood of Levi had been perfect at reconciling people to God, then Scripture would not have had to describe another priest according to the order of Melchizedek (instead of staying with the order of Aaron). If there is a need to change even one thing in the priesthood, it is obviously not perfect. It would indicate that other things, like the law, would need to be changed as well.

> *When we are able to defeat the angry enemy kings that rule in our mind, heart and things that are around us, Melchizedek (Priest of the Most High God) will also bless us.*

Melchizedek came from a different order and tribe that no one had ever served at God's holy altar before. Jesus descended from the tribe of Judah. However, Scripture never mentions a priest arising to serve from that tribe. Jesus is the only priest who resembles Melchizedek in so many ways. Jesus was not a priest because of some human lineage but because Jesus was sinless, the spotless Lamb of God, perfect inside and out. Jesus possessed the power of eternal life without end. *You are a priest forever—in the honored order of Melchizedek* (Psalm 110:4).

Because the earlier commandment had a weakness and did not reconcile us to God, it had to be set aside—after all, the law could not make anyone or anything perfect. Man did not possess the power to keep the law. God introduced a new and better hope that is centered in Jesus, the only true door. God swore an oath and confirmed this new covenant. It is only by entering into Jesus' resurrection power that we may draw near to God.

The Levite order of priests took office without an oath, while Jesus became a priest through God's oath. The Eternal One has sworn an oath and cannot change His mind: You are a priest forever. Jesus, the Son of God, permanently holds His priestly office. He lives forever; an eternal priest who will never have a successor! Jesus has become the guarantee of a new and better covenant (see Hebrews 7).

Our high priest is Jesus, the Alpha and Omega, the Beginning and the End. In Jesus, we find all that we need for life. And we find godliness that is centered in the power of His divine nature. God has a divine plan for an anointed rule of unity. He will exercise His royalty and unfailing purpose to reign supreme throughout all of time. When the final fulfillment of all the ages reaches its culmination, God will make All Things new, both in heaven and on earth, through the creative power of Jesus Christ, His Beloved Son (see Ephesians 1:10).

> *God the Father, as the wise vinedresser, graphs into the vine those who have committed their whole heart to Him so that they can bear eternal fruit that remains.*

Those who have spiritual ears hear what the Holy Spirit is saying; therefore, they are able to overcome and eat of the hidden manna. They receive a white stone with a new name written upon it, "IAM part of the One New Man" (see Revelation 2:17)! God knew all about us before we were even born, and His Spirit destined us from the beginning to share in the image and likeness of His Son. This means Jesus, the Son of God, is the oldest among a vast family of brothers and sisters who will become just like Him as part of the One New Man!

From the distant past, God's eternal love reached into the future to see you and me. In God's great foreknowledge, He knew those who would be His one day, so He chose them before the foundation of the world to be conformed into the image of His Son. God determined that Jesus would be the firstborn of a new family of Believers, all brothers and sisters. As for the sons and daughters God chose beforehand, He called them to a different destiny so that they would experience what it means to be made right with God and share as one in His glory. So never forget how you used to be. Jesus, the Great Preacher of peace and love, came for you. And His sweet voice found those of you who were near and those who were far away (see Ephesians 1:11, 17).

God's Holy Spirit desires to awaken us to the fact that Believers in Christ are called to form the One New Man.

Will everyone be a part of the One New Man? Sadly, no! Although each person is invited and called to become totally united as one in the Body of Christ, only the few, the remnant, will tune their ears to hear and repent, welcome the changes and do whatever is necessary to obediently answer the highest call. *So, the last will be first, and the first last. For many are called, but few chosen* (Matthew 20:16).

God the Father, as the wise vinedresser, graphs into the vine those who have committed their whole heart to Him so that they can bear eternal fruit that remains.

> Those of you born as outsiders to Israel were outcasts, branded *the uncircumcised* by those who bore the sign of the covenant in their flesh, a sign made with human hands. You had absolutely no connection to Christ the Anointed; you were strangers, separated from God's people. You were aliens to the covenant they had with God; you were hopelessly stranded without God in a fractured world. But now because of Jesus, the Anointed, and His sacrifice, all of that has changed. God gathered you who were so far away and brought you near to Him by the royal blood of Jesus the Anointed, our Liberating King. Jesus Christ is the embodiment of our peace, sent once and for all to take down the great barrier of hatred and hostility that has divided us so that we can be one with each other and one with Him.
>
> Jesus is the embodiment that brought out God's reconciling peace. He was sent by the Father once and for all to

> take down the great barriers of hate and hostile emotions so that we can become as one—Jew and non-Jew alike, male and female, young and old—Believers from every race, tribe and tongue joining together and being made equal through our union in and with Christ.
>
> Jesus offered His body, dying as a holy sacrifice on the cross to bring an end to the dictates of the law and its ordinances that separated Jews from the outside nations. Jesus having abolished in His flesh the enmity, that is, the law of commandments contained in ordinances, so as to create in Himself One New Man from the two, thus making peace. Jesus offered His body on the sacrificial altar to bring an end to the law's ordinances and dictations that separated Jews from the outside nations. Jesus' desire was to create within His body one new humanity from opposing groups with different traditions and beliefs in order to create peace. Two have now become one, and we live restored in God, reconciled in the unified Body of Christ. The cross was God's way of killing off hatred's hostility once and for all so that He is able to reconcile both Jew and Gentile to God in one united body (see Ephesians 1:11–16).

Through the power of the Holy Spirit dwelling within the One New Man, God is transforming each one of us into living temples not made of stone so that the Holy of Holies may become the Trinities dwelling place (see Ephesians 2:14–16, 22).

> By Him we also have access to the Father in one Spirit. And so, you are no longer called outcasts and wanderers but citizens with God's people, members of God's holy family, and residents of His household. You are being built on a solid foundation: the message of the prophets and the voices of God's chosen emissaries with Jesus, the Anointed Himself, the precious cornerstone. The building is joined together stone by stone—all of us chose, fitted together for a specific purpose and sealed in Him, rising up to become one holy temple in the Lord. In Christ, you are being built together as one, creating a sacred dwelling place among you where God Himself can live in the Spirit (see Ephesians 1:18–22).

God longs for the Spirit of Christ, who is presently dwelling in man, to abolish in His flesh the enmity, that is, the law of commandments contained in ordinances, so as to create in Himself One New Man from the two, thus making peace (see Ephesians 2:15).

God's Holy Spirit desires to awaken us to the fact that Believers in Christ are called to form the One New Man.

> *So, here is the result: as the sins of one man Adam brought about condemnation and punishment for all people, so Christ Jesus the one new man's act of faithfulness makes all of us right with God and brings us to new life as joint equal heirs in the One New Man* (Romans 5:18).

Let Us Pray

Dear Lord Jesus, I ask that You take up Your rightly place on the throne of my heart. Empower me to perceive, hear and see what You and Your Father are doing in heaven so that I can mirror it on earth. Give me Your grace so that I can slay all of my unlovely thoughts, attitudes and negative ideas. I ask that Your mighty hand of blessing would continually rest upon me. Make me new, and resurrect me by the power of Your Word. Prepare me to be a holy dwelling place that is fit for the Master's use. Amen.

CHAPTER FIFTEEN

The Power of Twelve

One boy's sacrificial meal of five loaves and two fishes increased and multiplied to the power of twelve to feed over five thousand men (women and children were not included in this number). Just like when Melchizedek blessed Abraham and Abraham increased and multiplied, when the bread and fish were blessed by Jesus (the sinless, perfect Priest giving God thanks for His provision), a miracle of multiplication took place.

When the few loaves and fishes were broken to be shared, the little boy's sacrifice supplied the needs of over twelve thousand people. When Jesus fed the thousands with one little boy's lunch, there was a powerful twelve thousandfold increase. The more Christlike we become, the more powerfully blessed and increased in favor we will be until every good thing that we touch or possess continually multiply in our lives.

One boy's bagged lunch x 1.5 = One man's (Jesus') serving portion of lunch x 5,000 men = 7,500 men fed, plus an additional 4,500 women and children = 12,000. Through imaginative prayer and thanksgiving, it is easy to get to a twelve thousandfold increase instead of settling for a meager thirty, sixty or one hundredfold increase, which represents the minimal levels of blessings. It is time to step into the thousandfold blessings of increase and multiplication *May the Lord, the God of your fathers, make you a thousand times as many as you are and bless you as He has promised you* (Deuteronomy 1:11)!

After the mass of people had eaten their fill, there were more leftovers collected in baskets than the original source of fish and bread they began with.

> *And Jesus took the five loaves and the two fish, and looking up to heaven, He blessed and broke and gave the loaves to the disciples; and the disciples gave to the multitudes. So, they all ate and were filled, and they took up twelve baskets full of the fragments that remained. Now those who had eaten were about five thousand men, besides women and children* (Matthew 14:19–21).

Twelve was the discipleship model that Jesus used to change the world. Jesus chose twelve apostles, the number of God's covenant elect purposes of God's power and authority. Even in our personal lives, no one can intimately invest in and personally relate to more than twelve friends at a time. Sometimes all we need to succeed is the company of twelve good, loyal friends. We should always be there for others. However, we should never sacrifice all of ourselves for only part of them in return.

Twelve represents the height of excellence in divine and human rulership under Creator God. The number twelve represents the following: the twelve judges; leadership; disciples or disciplines of the renewed mind (next chapter); apostolic fullness; divine government and apostolic order and rule (see Luke 6:12–13); creativity; illumination (see John 11:9); the Spirit world; plenty; twelve baskets of bread leftover; sons of Jacob; twelve stones of remembrance; Jesus' first recorded words; possession of the best; the twelve star constellations that represent the Twelve Apostles or the Twelve Tribes of Israel; Eden restored (see Revelation 12:1; 21:12–14); the twelve Holy Cities.

> *Twelve was the discipleship model that Jesus used to change the world.*

Sometimes a healing, a creative miracle, an increased harvest, the proliferation of finances to amass an abundance of wealth or the multiplication factor in God comes to us by quietly blowing our breath on a dying ember. At other times, expansion comes by simply surrendering our bagged lunch or changing the position of our net or network affiliations to the right or other side of the boat.

For forty years, heavenly manna rained down each morning upon Israel. The manna of God that fell fed Israel in the wilderness but spoiled after 24 hours (2 + 4 = 6). Six is the number of man. On Friday, the day before worship, the heavenly manna lasted for two days, 48 hours (4 + 8 = 12). Twelve is the number of Israel. When the manna was placed in the Holy of Holies in the wilderness tabernacle, it lasted over thousands of years.

Because gold is one of the most powerful conductors of energy that exists it covers the Ark of the Covenant. The Ark contained tablets of clay or stone and the gold jar of manna. The Ark of the Covenant was used by the priest to receive revelation knowledge as they traveled into heavenly dimensions.

The Levitical high priest would enter the Holy of Holies with a cord tied around one ankle. This leash insured that his body could be retrieved or removed from the Holy of Holies if he was not pure or made a mistake and was struck dead. To gain entrance through the veil, the priest placed his face on the thick material wall and then spoke the four-dimensional names of God. Miraculously, his whole body would be transported through the veil into the Holy of Holies to minister to God.

Sometimes a healing, a creative miracle, an increased harvest, the proliferation of finances to amass an abundance of wealth or the multiplication factor in God comes to us by quietly blowing our breath on a dying ember.

This miracle of provision of manna was followed with an invasion of multiplied thousands of flocks of quail landing in the evening to feed meat to millions of hungry people. Prophets express the meat of God's Word that illuminates what God is currently saying and doing at the moment. Prophets and seers are also used to speak forth what they see coming in the distant future so that we have time to readjust and realign with the Holy Spirit's plans and purposes.

God has formed and fashioned the Sons of God so that they can bring forth His manifest glory. The Sons of God are called to prophesy and foretell the future, do greater works and perform amazing signs, unusual wonders and peculiar, extraordinary creative miracles (see Acts 19:11).

> *Do not call to mind the former things, or ponder things of the past. Behold, I will do something new, now it will spring forth; will you not be aware of it? I will even make a roadway in the wilderness, rivers in the desert. The beasts of the field will glorify Me, the jackals and the ostriches, because I have given waters in the wilderness and rivers in the desert, to give drink to My chosen people. The people whom I formed for Myself will declare My praise* (Isaiah 43:18–21).

Jesus told us that we cannot have any life in us unless we eat or assimilate the eternal life that is found in the perfect flesh of the Son of Man (eat the bread that came down from heaven and drink of the redeeming merits of Jesus' precious, life-saving, healing blood). We must take on and possess His true body (as our daily food) and His genuine blood (as the drink) that sustains us in order to have eternal life and be raised up on the last day. If we daily eat of His flesh and drink of His blood, we will continue to dwell in His life-giving state of being.

Jesus' Father sent Him down to earth from an ascended heavenly place to dwell on earth. Jesus lived through His heavenly Father, who sustained Jesus from a higher realm of existence. If we continue to seek, love and focus (feed) on Jesus as our nourishing food, we will live eternally because the body and blood of Jesus is sustaining us here on earth from a higher realm in heaven. Jesus ascended in prayer to see what His Father was doing in heaven. Jesus knew that no man could come unto Him, to be transformed into eternal life, unless it was granted for him to do so by His Father. The Holy Spirit is the Word of Truth and the Giver of Life. The flesh is carnal; there is no profit or benefit within it whatsoever.

> God has formed and fashioned the Sons of God so that they can bring forth His manifest glory.

The crowd fell away when they realized Jesus was teaching that in order to have eternal life, we must take on the image and likeness of His body and healing saving power of His blood. We do not have the power or the ability to change others; we only have the power to change ourselves. Jesus knew from the beginning those who would believe, trust and place their faith in Him— would be the Believers who would obtain His eternal life. And Jesus also knew who would not be transformed by being born again but would betray Him unto His death on the cross.

Jesus turned and asked His disciples, "Will you also go and leave Me?" But Simon Peter replied, "Lord, to whom shall we go? You have the words of eternal life. The twelve of us have learned to trust and believe in You. We know that You are the Holy One of God, the Christ, the Anointed One, the Son of the Living God (see John 6:53–69).

The Sons of God are called to prophesy and foretell the future, do greater works and perform amazing signs, unusual wonders and peculiar, extraordinary creative miracles.

Jesus' final week of life was a time of cruel betrayal, bitter-sweet goodbyes and earthshaking powerful prayers as He prepared to freely lay down His life for the joy that was set before Him.

> *No one takes My life away from Me. On the contrary, I lay it down voluntarily. I release it from Myself into My Father's capable hands. I am authorized to resign my life for this purpose and I have power to lay My life down. I am also authorized and have power to take it back again. These are the instructed orders which I have received as My charge from My heavenly Father* (John 10:18).

All that the Father has given to Me I have kept secure and none is lost except Judas the Son of perdition (John 17:12).

Therefore, I sanctify, consecrate and dedicate Myself for My Believers sake that they may also be sanctified, consecrated to God and dedicated to holiness through the Spirit of Truth (John 17:19).

Let Us Pray

Dear Jesus, thank you that I am one of Your children. Help me to be more like the boy who shared all that he had with others. It was through his sacrificial gift of five loaves and fishes that he experienced the multiplication of miracle of provision in his life. After having given all he had, he received much more than his original source. Open my eyes to see, know and understand that You alone are my source of supply. Help me to know that You are all I need, because You are abundantly able to supply all of my needs according to Your riches in glory. Amen.

CHAPTER SIXTEEN

The Twelve Disciplines of the Imagination

Jesus foretold of the process of regeneration, where the Son of Man would ascend to sit on His throne of glory. Jesus prophesied that the people who followed Him would sit on twelve heavenly thrones to judge the Twelve Tribes of Israel. These Believers would eat and drink with Him at His bountiful table (see Matthew 19:28; Luke 22:30). Jesus is the prototype of the first man to take off corruptible flesh and put on an incorruptible, eternal body.

Believers in Christ are called to be quickened in the Spirit by taking off the limitations of the natural world's commonality. We must replace the carnal clothing of man's reasoning mind with the glories of the spiritual, incorruptible presence of God's immortality in order to have eternal life and possess victory over death (see Romans 1:23; 1 Corinthians 15:53–54). Through the Word of God that lives forever, we are able to step out of our mortal bodies and into the immortal Body of Christ, thus replacing everything that is subject to death with eternal life (see 1 Peter 1:18–23).

Jesus had His twelve apostles. Apostles are messengers of God who are sent forth as ambassadors to proclaim the spiritual thoughts of God on deliverance, healing and salvation. Apostles bring people into the baptism of cleansing that erases the negative powers of the mind and erroneous thoughts. *These twelve Jesus sent out and commanded them, saying: "Do not go into the way of the Gentiles, and do not enter a city of the Samaritans"* (Matthew 10:5). Jesus called His disciples friends, not slaves.

The lives of the Twelve Apostles of Jesus and the meanings of their names are a reflection of the qualities and attributes that our renewed mind should reflect.

> *And when Jesus had called His twelve disciples to Him, Jesus gave them power over unclean spirits, to cast them out, and to heal all kinds of sickness and all kinds of disease. Now the names of the twelve apostles are these: first, Simon, who is called Peter, and Andrew his brother; James the son of Zebedee, and John his brother; Philip and Bartholomew; Thomas and Matthew the tax collector; James the son of Alphaeus, and Lebbaeus, whose surname was Thaddaeus; Simon the Canaanite, and Judas Iscariot, who also betrayed Jesus* (Matthew 10:1–4).

The Twelve Disciples of Jesus can communicate different giftings that represent various faculties and spiritual dimensions or creative, righteous ideas we need to adopt in order to renew our mind in Christ. As you read through the following descriptions of the Twelve Disciples, consider your own attributes in comparison. Jesus specifically chose each of these apostles to join Him during His ministry on earth.

Simon Peter—Simon Peter (means *a hearing; God heard; diligent;* see Psalm 61:5) was known as the ROCK, the unmovable disciple with powerful faith. Peter could not be influenced, coerced or swayed by any words he heard. Hearing suggestions that reach our consciousness will cause them to come into being. Peter discovered Christ as the IAM, so he was given the keys of the Kingdom.

Peter made bold, heavenly declarations that loosed the lawful on earth and bound the improper, unlawful things. *You are Peter and, on this rock,* (of revelation) *I will build my church, and the powers of death shall not prevail against it* (Matthew 16:18). Peter represents the brain that has centered his faith in Jesus as Messiah God and the spiritual discernment of All Things.

Moses commanded us to keep the law; as part of our godly heritage as the people of the congregation of Jacob (Deuteronomy 33:4).

You have ignored and been unmindful of the Rock "Christ" who bore you and have forgotten God the Father who gave you spiritual birth (Deuteronomy 32:18).

> Moses said to God, "Please, show me Your glory, for I want to see You." God declared to Moses, "I will make all of My goodness pass right in front of you, and I will proclaim the names of the Lord before you. I'll call out the glorious names of God in your presence. I will be gracious to whom I will be gracious and treat them with kindness. I will have compassion on whom I will have compassion." But He said, "Moses, you cannot see My face until you are born again from above; for no earthly, carnal man shall see Me and live." And the Lord said, "Look now, Moses (means to be born or drawn from the water), for here is a place that I have created for you that is right beside Me. But you must choose to put yourself on this rock, to stand on the rock by Me. So it shall be, while the goodness of My glory passes by, that I will put you in the cleft of the rock, to conform you to My image, and I will cover you with My hand while I pass by. Then I will take away My hand, and you shall see My back (that bore the healing stripes for man's rebirth into salvation); but My face shall not be seen by you" (see Exodus 33:18–23).

When we are able to go all the way back to understand that our beginning and end is within Christ, we will be converted into becoming part of the One New Man Christ, thus seeing His glorious face.

There is no one who is holy like the Eternal LORD, for there is none besides You, nor is there any Rock as solid and true as our God (1 Samuel 2:2).

Who is the True God except the Eternal One the Lord? Who stands like a rock except our God (2 Samuel 22:32)?

And all will drink of the same spiritual drink. For they drank spiritual water from a spiritual Rock that followed them Christ was always with them. For the Rock was the Anointed One, our own Liberating King, Christ Jesus the Lord (1 Corinthians 10:4).

Jesus represents the head of the Body of Christ. Jesus ascended to the top of the mountain to pray and visit with His heavenly Father. He was crucified on the head or the place of the skull (Golgotha). For each of us to ascend the prayer mountain to reach God (to see His glory), we must be pressed into the same mold or image in order to become of the same spirit as the Rock, Jesus. We must be born again by the Spirit and water in order for the eyes in our blind skull to see and know God.

The ministry of death, written and engraved on stones, was so glorious that the children of Israel could not behold or look steadily on the face of Moses even as the glory was passing from his countenance (2 Corinthians 3:7).

And as Jesus prayed, the fashion of His countenance was changed to that of lightning, and His clothing was shone forth as brilliant white snow (see Luke 9:29; Matthew 28:3).

Jesus had in His right hand seven stars, out of His mouth went a sharp two-edged sword, and His countenance was like the sun shining in its strength (Revelation1:16).

Jesus is the One who shows us the ways of life, so it is He who will make us full of joy when His countenance rests upon us (Acts 2:28).

For the Lord is righteous, He loves righteousness; His countenance beholds the upright (Psalm 11:7).

Blessed are the people who know the joyful sound! They walk, O Lord, in the light of Your countenance (Psalm 89:15).

Andrew—Andrew (means *manly; enduring trust in the divine; a courageous, spiritually strong man of strength and mental stability*) represents a daring, resolute valor and enduring faith in God that makes oneself brave and confident enough to bring others to Jesus Christ. Be brave and strong, don't give up, put on the whole armor of God. Draw your strength and might from God. Let your heart be a courageous tower all you who place your hope in the Lord and in His mighty power (see Psalm 31:24; Ephesians 6:10).

Andrew saw the Lord as his light and salvation, the strength of his life, so he was not afraid (see Psalm 27:1). Andrew was a disciple of John the Baptist and a fisherman. He brought the lad with the five loaves to Jesus. Andrew preached the gospel in Greece and Scythia, and he brought the Greeks to Jesus. Andrew suffered martyrdom (at Patrae in Achaia) on an X shaped cross. The unseen claims of the Believer are sustained by faith, while the faith of the undisciplined man cannot be seen. Andrew knew the truth and was not silent about the good news. He dared to bring others to Christ. Andrew was known as the strongman that represents strength and the power that is found in the loins. Gaza means physical citadel of strength; it refers to the loins.

> *Jesus asked two of John the Baptist's disciples who started following Him, "What do you want?" They responded, "Rabbi* (means master or teacher), *where are you staying?" Jesus answered, "Come and discover for yourselves." So, they went with Him and saw where He was staying, and since it was late in the afternoon, they spent the rest of the day with Jesus. One of the two disciples who heard and declared John's words, "There's God's Lamb!" was a man named Andrew, and he began to follow Jesus. Andrew went and found his brother, Simon, and told him, "We have found the Anointed One* (the Christ)*!" Then Andrew brought Simon to meet Jesus. When Jesus gazed upon Andrew's brother, he prophesied to him, "You are Simon, and your father's name is John. But from now on you will be called Cephas* (means Peter the Rock)*"* (John 1:38–42).

James—James was the just, righteous judge who was blindfolded so that he did not follow the flesh or natural appearances of circumstances. James forgave people for their actions. James used his gift of prophesy to bless others by telling people what gives them joy. The name James comes from Jacob. James, the son of Zebedee, represents the wisdom of choice in important, life-changing matters (like who to marry). James represents the spiritual intuition that helps us to determine right from wrong and to obtain quick knowing and discrimination of outer forces or good judgment when dealing with life-changing matters. James, as one of the sons of thunder, represents strong emotions that are tied to gut feelings, which takes up his residence in the pit of the stomach. James, the first martyr among the apostles, was beheaded by the order of King Herod Agrippa.

John—John the Beloved (means *God is gracious; the strength of God*) rested his head on the chest of Jesus. He was Jesus' best friend. John promoted love instead of hate. John's actions inspire us to respond to adversity in a nonviolent manner. If we encourage others to reach the greatness that is resident within them, they will honor, love and respect us. If we judge, condemn or criticize others, they will shy away and vanish from our lives forever. We all face adverse difficulties in life that help to mold a strong, godly character. If you want to know what someone is truly made of, give him power. Then watch to see if he sets the captives free, heals the broken-hearted and builds others up, or, in contrast, if he takes people captive, enslaving them by destroying their rights to freedom of speech and liberty.

John was entrusted with the care of Jesus' mother, Mary. John the Beloved represents love that dwells in the heart of the Believer. Jerusalem is the throne of love. John was a fisherman born at Bethsaida. After the ascension, he, Peter and James were in charge of the Jerusalem Church. After he moved to Ephesus, John the Revelator became the head of the churches in Asia Minor. John was banished to the barren island of Patmos by the Roman emperor.

Phillip—Phillip (means *lover of horses; transformed*) wanted to see the perfect likeness or image of God the Father in an awakened state of being. *We all with unveiled face, beholding in a mirror the glory of the Lord, are being transformed into the same image from glory to glory* (2 Corinthians 3:18). Horses represent power of the flesh. Philip represents the power of the spoken Word of God that is rooted in the tongue that governs and controls the vibrations of the larynx and vocal cords, the mind, body and taste.

Jesus taught His disciples as One who had great authority. And Jesus came and spoke to them, saying, *"All power is given unto Me in heaven* (the renewed mind) *and on earth* (the renewed body) (Matthew 28:18)".

Power takes many forms. Patience is power when it is linked with the right, timely actions taken for the right purposes, with godly principles and executed in love. I believe in the immeasurable power of God's unending love, for His far-reaching, all-encompassing love is true. God's love empowers us to overcome any circumstance by prayerfully removing mountains of opposition.

Never underestimate the power of love, a gentle caring touch, a sweet, warm smile, a kind word in season, a steady listening ear, an honest compliment or a considerate, kind act; for these have great potential to transform a life into something beautiful.

We have each been given one life to live, so accept the power to choose wisely, speak kindly and live well. Choose to take the high, narrow road that is less traveled, then walk it with dignity. No one else can make your life choices for you. Choose to exercise the power that has been given to you to make your life happy and full.

The Hebrew letter *Pey* represents the mouth. The words we speak hold the transforming power of life or death. We are able to bind things on earth that are bound in heaven and loose things on earth that are loosed in heaven. Our words have the power to create a new heaven and new earth.

> *I saw a new heaven and a new earth, for the old heaven and the old earth had disappeared. And the sea was also gone. Then I, John, saw the holy city, the new Jerusalem, coming down from God out of heaven like a bride beautifully dressed for her husband. I heard a loud shout from the throne, saying, "Look, God's home is now among His people! He will live with them, and they will be His people. God Himself will be with them. He will wipe every tear from their eyes, and there will be no more death or sorrow or crying or pain. All these things are gone forever." And the One sitting on the throne said, "Look, I am making everything new!" And then He said to me, "Write this down, for what I tell you is trustworthy and true"* (Revelation 21:1–5).

By exercising the spiritual dominion of the divine mind over the body, great power is released, producing signs, wonders and miracles. Jesus made it clear that He was from above and that His kingdom was not of this world. He stated that both heaven and earth will pass away, but His Words will by no means pass away. His eternal Spirit gives and brings life to us, for His Words are Spirit and life. The flesh has nothing to offer, so it profits us nothing (see Matthew 24:35; John 6:63).

Mentioned as the fifth of the twelve, Apostle Philip was a native to Bethsaida. He was an evangelist and a deacon at the Jerusalem Church. He preached in Samaria. Phillip was directed by an angel (see Acts 8:26) to go south from Jerusalem to Gaza where he found, preached to, saved and baptized the Ethiopian traveler. Phillip was married and had four virgin daughters, who prophesied to the people.

> *No man at any time has seen the Father, but I have seen Him. When you see Me, you have seen the Father for I and my Fa-*

> *ther are one. If anyone resolutely believes in Me, he will be able to do the things that I do; and even greater things than these, because I go to the Father. If you really love Me, you will keep and obey My commands and you will be loved by My Father and I will also love him. I will show, reveal, and manifest Myself to him. Letting Myself be clearly seen by him. I will make Myself real to him. And I will ask the Father, and He will give you another Comforter, Counselor, Helper, Intercessor, Advocate, Strengthener, and Standby, that He may remain with you forever—The Spirit of Truth, whom the world cannot receive into their heart, because it does not see Him, know or recognize Him. But you know and recognize Truth, for He constantly lives with you and will be in you* (John 14:8–21).

Bartholomew—Bartholomew (means heir) was the son of Tomai. He became an apostle after Jesus' death and resurrection (see Matthew 10:3; Acts 1:13). *Giving thanks to the Father, who has qualified us to share in the inheritance of the saints in light* (Colossians 1:12). He represents the separation of the kernel of wheat from the chaff.

Educated people often fail because of a lack of imagination; they conform and become followers instead of being leaders. If your life inspires others to imagine, to dream the impossible dream and to learn to do more so that they become more, you are a leader. Bartholomew is connected to the soul that represents the creative power of the imagination. It is found between the eyes reaching back into the brain to create amazing visions, project images, display ideas and generate pictures.

Bartholomew was called Nathanael in John 1, where Jesus saw his beautiful, guileless spirit come into focus before his physical body, resting under the fig tree, came into view. The fig tree is a symbol of Israel. Figs represent peace, prosperity, solitude and the communion with God that brings forth provision and health. The visual images that entered into Jesus' mind gave His imagination the ability to interpret their meanings.

The Spirit of Truth guided Jesus to rightly discern the truth about a person's character. Jesus was able to look past the veil of the natural to see the truth hidden in the heart of an individual. As we learn to correctly interpret symbolism to behold the glory of the Lord in our imagination, His truth will transform us into His same image from glory to glory.

Thomas—Thomas (means *divinely preserved twin*) was called Didymus the Twin. Discretion will guard you; understanding will watch over you (Proverbs 2:11). Thomas (at first) doubted and denied Christ. He could not believe in the resurrection of Christ without physical evidence. But when Thomas became believing, he denied that sickness had any power to afflict him and resisted all suggestions of negative impressions.

Thomas represents the understanding, reasoning and intellectual perception that is found in the front of the brain. True spiritual understanding empowers the Believer to realize that the resurrection of a dead body back to life is not restricted to Jesus alone. Because he spoke out and questioned things, Thomas is known as the doubter. He wanted to discover, understand and know everything.

Jesus knew that He was the light of the world. He continually honored the Father in all He said and did. Jesus never tried to get anything for Himself. He always gave all the glory to God. Jesus spoke with absolute confidence when He declared: *I tell you the truth, anyone who hears My voice, practices what IAM telling you and keeps My Word will never experience death* (John 8:51). Speaking is Believing! Speaking, praying, prophesying and decreeing a thing precedes seeing!

> *The other disciples kept telling Thomas, "We have seen the Lord!" But he said to them, "Unless I see in His hands the marks made by the nails and put my finger into the nail prints, and put my hand into His side, I will never believe." Eight days later Jesus came, behind the closed doors, and stood among them and said, "Peace to you!" He said to Thomas, "Reach out your finger here, and see My hands; and put out your hand and place it in My side. Do not be faithless and incredulous, but stop your unbelief and believe!" Thomas answered Him, "My Lord and my God!" Jesus said to him, "Because you have seen Me, Thomas, do you now believe, trust, have faith? Blessed and happy and to be envied are those who have never seen Me and yet have believed, adhered to and trusted in and relied on Me"* (John 20:24–29).

Matthew—Matthew (means *gift of God; one who gives honor back to God*) worked as a tax collector before he followed Jesus. His original name, when he was a publican, was Levi. Matthew was present in the upper room at Jerusalem after Christ's ascension. Every desire of Matthew's heart was a gift from heaven. *Bless the Lord, O my soul. O Lord my God, You are very great; You are clothed with honor and majesty* (Psalm 104:1). Matthew represents the overcoming will of man, which is located in the center front of the brain. He suffered martyrdom in Ethiopia.

> *Assuredly I say to you, that in the regeneration when creation is consummated and All Things are renewed, when the Son of Man sits on His throne in glory, you who have followed Me will also sit on thrones. There will be twelve thrones, and you will sit and judge the twelve tribes of Israel* (Matthew 19:28).

James—James (means *nurtured; supplanter*) had clear discrimination, good judgment and spiritual discernment. He judged by the Spirit's intuition, not from a natural rule of law. James had vibrant prophetic insights into the mysteries of God. James, the son of Alphaeus, is represented in the navel or pit of the stomach where quick knowing takes place. He aligned himself with God's divine order; he centered his being in the middle of Christ's manifest presence. *Yea, though I walk through the valley of the shadow of death, I will fear no evil; for thou art with me; thy rod and thy staff they comfort me* (Psalm 23:4).

> Count it all joy when you encounter every sort of trial and various temptations. Trials prove your faith, bringing out endurance and steadfast patience. Let patience do a thorough work so that you are perfected and fully developed in Christ, lacking nothing. If you need wisdom, ask God for it. He will give liberally and without reproach or faultfinding. Always ask in focused faith, not wavering, hesitating or doubting like a surging wave on the sea that is tossed by the wind. If you doubt, you will be unstable, unreliable and uncertain in all of your ways; you will not receive anything from the Lord. Every good and perfect gift comes down from the Father of Light in whom there is no shadow variance or turning (see James 1:1–17).

Thaddaeus—Thaddaeus (means *loving; joyful*) was the tenth disciple. Because he gave God thanksgivings for the spiritual gifts and resources that he was given and received, he was known as the disciple of praise. *The*

Lord is my strength and my shield; my heart trusted in Him, and I am helped; therefore, my heart greatly rejoices, and with my song I will praise Him (Psalm 28:7). Ten lepers were cleansed, but only one was made whole. The one was made whole when he came back to give Jesus thanks.

Thaddaeus represents denial, renunciation or eliminating error, so it is tied to the abdominal region that deals with the elimination of waste through the bowels.

> *The Good News has been announced to you by those who preached in the power of the Holy Spirit sent from heaven. It is all so wonderful that even the angels are eagerly watching these things happen. Therefore, gird up the loins of your mind,* (the imaginative, reproductive, creative part of your abdomen to birth a new identity) *be sober, self-controlled and rest your hope fully upon the grace and salvation that is to be brought to you at the revelation of Jesus Christ; as obedient children, not conforming yourselves to the former lusts, as in the ignorance of your old carnal ways. But live holy as unto the Lord* (1Peter 1:13.)

Simon—Simon of Canaan (means *God heard; hearing; receptivity*), the eleventh disciple, was the man with the pitcher of water that lead the other disciples to the Last Supper or The Feast of the Passover. Simon had the ability to hear good news and leave the negative behind. He was kind of heart. Simon stayed focused on being of a noble consciousness.

Simon was one who maintained a dignified nature in order to enjoy the abundant life; he ate at a lavish banquet table that had been prepared in the presence of his enemies. *For You, O God, have heard my vows; You have given me the heritage of those who fear, revere, and honor Your name* (Psalm 61:5).

Simon represents one who is diligent to listen to truth with an open, renewed, Christlike mind in order to develop a greater measure of faith. Faith is formed and expressed in the silence of one's heart. The spoken Word by way of verbal prayer, declaration and decree becomes a creative force, as it actives the Spirit's power.

Simon the Canaan also represents the zeal that comes when one hears and receives God's Word with faith. Simon was known as the zealot because he was totally consumed with God. He had a healthy respect for the Eternal.

> *God, my life is an open book to You. You know every foolish sin I've ever committed. For nothing within me is hidden from Your sight! Lord Yahweh of angel armies, keep me from ever being a stumbling block to others who wait for You, or to those who love You. Lord God of Israel, don't let what happens to me be the source of confusion that would confound those who passionately seek for You. Because of my love for You, Lord, I have borne reproach, been mocked, cursed, and disgraced. Even my own brothers, those of my family, act as though I am a stranger to them. They are ashamed of me and don't want anything to do with me. My love for You has my heart on fire! My passion consumes me for Your house! Zeal for Your house has eaten me up! Nothing will turn me away, even though I endure all the insults of those who insult You* (Psalm 69:5–12).

Simon was completely devoted to protecting God's house. Some people have zeal for God, but it is not based on true biblical knowledge, so it does not lead them to Him (see Romans 10:2). Zeal takes up its residence at the back of the head and rests in the medulla at the base of the brain.

The pineal gland is located at the center of your brain, above the cerebellum, and it functions as the spiritual faith center of the brain. The pineal gland generates serotonin that governs your energy, mood levels of happiness and confidence to achieve. The pineal also generates Dimethyltryptamine (DMT), a hallucinogenic visionary substance that creates spiritual vision. To promote a healthy pineal gland, include pressed virgin coconut oil in your diet, eat raw Cacao beans and other healthy raw, organic foods, detox with apple cider vinegar, sit in the sun's light to generate higher serotonin levels and drink a small amount of iodine in purified water to flush out sodium fluoride and to support healthy thyroid function.

Take your everyday, ordinary life—your sleeping, eating, going-to-work, and walking-around life—and place it before God as an offering. Don't copy the behavior and customs of this world to fit into a culture that will mold you into the world's image. Instead, fix your attention on God. Become a new person who is transformed from the inside out into a different, better, mature person, who thinks the higher thoughts of God, until you are satisfied and able to discern the good, pleasing and complete will of God (see Romans 12:2). Taking on the mind of Christ empowers us to think mature spiritual thoughts, adapting the ways of God (see Philippians 3:15).

Judas—Judas (means *praised; full of love*) represents the disciplined aspect of detachment from the world, letting go of all that is known. Judas was the son of Simon, surnamed Iscariot. The world rejected Judas because of his theft, selfishness and greed in betraying Jesus and his friends for thirty pieces of silver, the price of a slave, and also because he committed suicide. But God lays down His life for His friends. *I give you a new commandment: that you should love one another. Just as I have loved you, so you too should love one another* (John 13:34).

Judas represents betrayal and selfish greed that drains one's life energy. He represents being governed by pleasure or sexual sensation. He also represents one who conserves or governs the life's consciousness and generative, procreative functions in the body's life. After the Lord's Supper, Judas led the temple guard and raging mob to the Garden of Gethsemane. He kissed Christ's face as his signal to take Jesus hostage. He later repented to the chief priest for his sin of betrayal of innocent blood and tried to return the thirty silver pieces. He hung himself on the hillside of the Valley of Hinnom called Aceldama.

Did any of these characteristics, attributes or disciplines resonate with you? It is wise to consider what attributes are good and pleasing to the Lord so that you may prove yourself worthy of your calling or destiny.

The Twelve Tribes of Israel

There were twelve sons born to Jacob (Israel). Let's continue our exploration of the significance of twelve with the consideration of the attributes and characteristics of the Twelve Tribes of Israel. As you may recall, we learned (Volume II) that each tribe was assigned to one of the twelve constellations.

It is said that the Red Sea split in twelve different paths to provide a separate life journey for each of the Twelve Tribes of Israel. They traveled together as twelve separate tribes, and they repeated their same offerings of dedication to the temple twelve times. At the end of the Torah, Moses also blessed the Twelve Tribes of Israel (see Deuteronomy 33:6–25). The Tribes of Israel were named by their mothers (see Genesis 29–30; 35:18), and Jacob blessed each of his twelve sons before he passed away.

Rueben—The First. Rueben was born in the month of Tammuz, a time of devoted worship—where we are to review the events of our life as if they were individual photos in a filmstrip. Reuben's name means *a wondrous recognition* and *behold or see the difference in my son* (see Genesis 29:32). Rueben, was the foremost son to Jacob, so he had great privilege, strength, might and power of excellence. He would have inherited a double portion. Jacob prophesied over Rueben, "You are my firstborn, my might, the beginning of my strength, the excellency of my dignity, the excellency of power. Unstable as water, you shall not excel."

Rueben had great potential, but he lost the firstborn son rights, just as Esau lost (sold) his to Jacob. Yet Reuben's response to the actions of his little brother, Joseph, was not one of murder, unlike his siblings'. Rueben fought to save Joseph in his time of need when his jealous brothers sought to kill him. Rueben did not resent Joseph; he tried to protect him.

Rueben represents the power that comes from being the first. Like the energy force of water that can flow either way, he was unstable. If water is channeled correctly, it produces life through irrigation, and it generates electrical power. If this power is left unchecked, it will flood and erode all boundaries, leaving a wake of destruction in its path.

Rueben was highly tuned and could see through his certain, immediate awareness of God. Rueben tried to gain family power by sleeping with Jacob's concubine Bilhah. When Jacob learned of his deceptive ploy, he cursed Rueben (see Genesis 35:21–22). Reuben settled for a section of land ruled by Sihon and Og. The portion of land was outside of the Promised Land, so his tribe was the first to be captured.

Simeon—The Aggressor. Simeon, the second son of Jacob and Leah, had a fierce, cruel anger. When unbridled, he released his wrath as a weapon of violence to consume everyone who crossed his path. His name means *diligent, to hear* and *God has heard. For you have heard my vows, O God; You have given me the inheritance of th–se who fear Your name* (Psalm 61:5).

Levi—The Cleric. Levi was the third son of Jacob and Leah. *For you will light my lamp; the Lord my God will enlighten my darkness* (Psalm 18:28).

His name means attached or joined. Levi was chosen by God, and he dedicated his life to serve a higher calling in the Temple. Levi was able to let go of all earthly, material goods and longings in order to bond himself to the divine service of God. However, Levi did join with Simeon's violence in massacring the men of Shechem.

Judah—The Leader (on the path to selflessness). The name Judah means *let God be praised* (see Genesis 29:35). David took out Goliath, casting a smooth stone against his enemy. Judah was the fourth son of Jacob and Leah. An acknowledgement of God is worthy to be praised. His descendants became the kings of Israel. Jacob prophesied over Judah that his brothers would praise him. The word Jew came from Judah, which has to do with the justice found in law.

Issachar—The Scholar. Issachar's name means *a righteous reward God has given me* and *my hired wages* (see 1 Samuel 24:19). Issachar was the fifth son of Leah and ninth of Jacob. Issachar knew and understood the times and the prophetic timing and wisdom of events to give Israel a clear strategy and direction in order to be successful, advance and prosper (see 1 Chronicles 12:32). He was dedicated to studying. Education is foundational for any organization, corporation or family unit to prosper. Jacob prophesied that Issachar was a strong donkey because he was a servant who could bear much, lying down or standing between two burdens.

Zebulun—The Businessperson. The name Zebulun means *habitation.* He was the sixth son Leah and tenth of Jacob. Zebulun made his living as a merchant of the marketplace; he redeemed the treasures found in people and in the material, natural world (see Deuteronomy 33:19). Zebulun supports the scholar Issachar (from the trade produced from the ware on the sea bringing them to shore) so that he can glean from his great wisdom on timing for purchases, mergers and acquisitions. These two make great business partners.

Dan—The Judge (on the path of law and order that brings justice to society). The name Dan means *God is my discerning judge* (see Psalm 119:42). Dan was the last tribe to receive its territorial inheritance. Dan was the fifth son of Jacob and first of Bilhah, Rachel's maid. Dan was part of a loose confederation of Israelite tribes. No central government existed, and in times of crisis, the people were led by leaders (like Samson) known as judges.

The Tribe of Dan was a seafaring group that joined the new kingdom with Saul as the first king. After the death of Saul, all the tribes other than Judah remained loyal to the House of Saul. However, after the death of Ishbosheth, Saul's son and successor to the throne of Israel, the Tribe of Dan joined the other northern Israelite tribes in making David king over Judah. Dan provided substantial expert military support.

Dan is depicted by "scales of justice" and "(Dan) shall achieve justice for his kindred" (see Genesis 49:16). Others use a snake to represent Dan. *Let Dan be a serpent by the roadside, a horned viper by the path, that bites the horse's heel, so that the rider tumbles backward* (Genesis 49:17).

Naphtali—The Free Spirit. Naphtali was the second son of Bilhah and sixth of Jacob. Naphtali means *a doe let loose*, and the symbol of the tribe is a gazelle. He reflects the beauty of a wild deer leaping, showing us that "our struggle" for independence and exploration is essential for growth.

The people of Naphtali are traditionally thought of as communicators, swift runners with goodly words. Naphtali was one of the ten lost tribes and was one of the northernmost of the Twelve Tribes of Israel. Joshua assigned Naphtali the eastern side of the Galilee. Naphtali was known for their military expertise.

Gad—The Warrior. Gad's name means *a troop of fortune comes* or *how fortunate* (see Genesis 30:10–11). Gad depicts a person of *luck* who is ready to take up arms as a soldier and fight for his or her personal beliefs or for what is just and right. Gad cherishes godly values and freedoms.

Gad settled on the eastern side of the Jordan. Moses was buried in the territory of Gad. The Prophet Elijah may have been a descendant of Gad. Known as the seer, Gad was the seventh son of Jacob and first of Zilpah, Leah's maid. Jacob prophesied over Gad, "A raiding troop shall raid him, but he shall raid at their heels and victoriously assault them."

Asher—The Prosperous One. The name Asher means *happy, fortunate and blessed* (see Psalm 16:11). Asher, the eighth son of Jacob and second of Zilpah, was the happy one. Asher deals with the abundance of blessings and pleasures of prosperity so that one has enough to give to every good work. Asher is an abundant provider.

Joshua assigned Asher the coastal western portion of Galilee. This region had humid temperatures and a great deal of rainfall, so it was the most fertile land (rich pastures, wooded hills and orchards) in Canaan. Asher was particularly prosperous and known for its olive oil. Jacob prophesied over Asher that his food would be rich.

Benjamin—The Ravenous Consumer. Benjamin's name means *mighty son of my right hand* (see Psalm 18:35). Benjamin was the twelfth and youngest son of Jacob and second of Rachel, who died after giving birth to him. Rachel named him Benoni (son of my sorrow), but Jacob renamed him as his beloved son, "the son of my strength, the son of my right hand".

Benjamin was always hungry for the divine presence of God. Jacob prophesied, "Benjamin is a ravenous wolf. In the morning he shall devour the prey, and at night he shall divide the spoil.". His passionate pursuit of God's energy caused him to be elevated by Joseph and dearly loved by Israel. Moses described Benjamin as "dwelling between YHWH's shoulders".

Joseph—The Sufferer. Joseph's name means *he will add.* He was the eleventh son of Jacob and the first of Rachel. His father, Israel, loved Joseph more than all of his other children, for Joseph was the son of his old age. Israel made and clothed Joseph with a distinctive, colorful tunic with sleeves (see Genesis 37:3). Jacob prophesied over Joseph that he would be a fruitful bough, faithful and fruitful. Joseph not only survived but also thrived in opposition and oppression. Because God was with him, he always rose to the top as an expert national leader.

Joseph was sold to the Ishmaelites for twenty pieces of silver and was carried to Egypt, where he became governor over all the land. His greatness was found in his spiritual imagination that interpreted dreams and moral integrity, which enabled him to escape calculated situations of unjust sabotage and death threats to save a nation from famine and the world from starvation.

Joseph had two sons, Manasseh and Ephraim, who were birthed after his time of dark persecution and affliction.

Manasseh—Reconnection. Manasseh was Joseph's first born, and his name means *I will forget* and *negation* (to forget and forgive). Manasseh represented Joseph's ability to overcome the worldly or occult powers of Egypt, which attempted to expel one's belief in one God!

Ephraim—Transformation. The name Ephraim means *an ability to give affirmation* and *to be doubly fruitful* and *to multiply in a land full of affliction.* Although Ephraim, Joseph's second son by his wife Asenath, was younger than his brother Manasseh, he was regarded with special favor. Ephraim represents the power to transform the process of overcoming difficulties into an ability to receive God's divine power.

The difficulties in life develop our faith and degree of trust that is needed to keep the measure of our spirit growing and expanding. If we treat people with honor and respect and go the extra mile, we will always be out in front of the crowd. Learn to focus your attentions on magnifying God to receive the solution, not on the difficulty or problem at hand.

Israel—Reminder. The name Israel means *the prince that wrestles and prevails with God.* Jacob, the Prince of Israel, reminds us that each one of us will have to wrestle with God at Peniel to be transformed into a new person, taking on a new name and identity in Christ in order to walk in the ways and truth of God (see Genesis 32:25).

Personal Reflection Moment

1. Do you see yourself in any of these men?
2. Which of these twelve life paths have you decided to journey on?
3. What are the strengths that you have in common with these men?
4. What weaknesses do you display that need to be worked on, repented of and overcame by the grace of God?

Sometimes we can learn of the ways of God by relating to someone who is greater than us, asking him or her to serve as our mentor, coach or life example. We can discover how to grow spiritually by emulating him or her. We can ascertain knowledge from others' experiences and glean from their wisdom, thus we can arrive at their station in life in a shorter measure of time than it took them to arrive.

Let Us Pray

Dear Lord Jesus, I want to be one of Your faithful disciples who follow You in everything that You say and do. Help me to take off the corruptible flesh and put on an incorruptible, eternal body. Quicken me by the Holy Spirit so that I can take off the limitations of the natural world's commonality. Replace my carnal mind and earthly reasoning with the glories of the Holy Spirit's renewed mind and presence. Show me where my weak attributes are so that I can repent and put on Your strengths. Amen.

CHAPTER SEVENTEEN

Multiplication and Advancement

Vision causes a God-given, supernatural strength to arise from within our being. Vision empowers us to surmount every mental stronghold and conquer every physical and spiritual giant. Do not take old thought patterns or outdated ways of doing things into a new season of prosperity; their usefulness has expired, and they will no longer work.

Prosperity is a gradual process that involves addition, increase and finally culminates in multiplication. We slowly evolve taking on more influence, strength and stature until we are able to stand up under the weight of God's goodness and sustain all of His blessings. It is time to gain the wisdom that is needed to restore our fortunes. *Turn us back to You, O Lord, and we will be restored; renew our days as of old* (Lamentations 5:21). Expect to receive new directions that will set your emotions free in order to restore your fortunes that have been held up in captivity.

> *When the Lord brought back the captive ones of Zion, we were like those who dream. Then our mouth was filled with laughter and our tongue with joyful shouting; then they said among the nations, "The Lord has done great things for them." The Lord has done great things for us; we are glad. Restore our captivity, O Lord, as the streams in the South. Those who sow in tears shall reap with joyful shouting. He who goes to and fro weeping, carrying his bag of seed, shall indeed come again with a*

shout of joy, bringing his sheaves with him (Psalm 126).

Ask God to help you see the needs of others. Pray for vision to see what you have in your hand (skill set) or what kind of provision you have to solve that need. Don't grumble, complain or curse your provision with doubt and unbelief. Take what you have in your hand, give thanks and bless it so that you can learn how to add to, enlarge, prosper and understand how godly provision multiplies.

Develop a budget. Do not squander your profit on foolish passing pleasures. Learn to save money, and live below your means; therefore, you will have seed to invest in every good work. Sowing into kingdom projects will cause your own finances to increase and multiply. Invest the interest you earn from your resources back into your own ventures. Then purchase real estate, or start a new business to hire and retain others to work for you.

> *We slowly evolve taking on more influence, strength and stature until we are able to stand up under the weight of God's goodness and sustain all of His blessings.*

Develop marketplace skills through training and instruction that will position you for promotion. Have a mindset to grow and market your creative abilities. Multiply through creativity to form a larger profit margin to invest in and prosper from the invention of more products.

Discipline yourself to daily give God your best time. Sit at Jesus' feet, and focus your attention on His words. Listen to Jesus' heart to gain His wisdom. Tapping into God's foreknowledge will give you the necessary strategy to multiply what you have already accomplished in a smaller amount of time. Jesus prospered in every situation. Jesus conquered death! The resurrection power of God entered hell to take captivity captive. Jesus delivered all of those souls from the power of death. Jesus carried the saints with Him into eternal freedom.

We are to fight from a position of victory to victory and to continually rejoice with thanksgiving in order to bring forth that same dimension of resurrection power that releases multiplication in our lives. God has compassion on us when we have lack. God's wisdom will give us a plan to prosper when we tithe, give alms and give our first fruits offerings. Always give thanks for the little crumb, and bless the penny you find on the ground. Then pray for increase, prosperity and multiplication until the loaf of bread and the dollar bills appear. Give thanks, and continue to pray until the bakery shows up to feed the multitudes and the bank becomes evident to finance the advancement of God's Kingdom.

Jacob's Spotted and Speckled Prosperity

Believers adopt the higher thoughts and glorious ways of Christ that have been birthed within our sanctified imagination. Before we recognize and apprehend all that God has done for us, evil and the darkness of the world is able to take advantage. *But this is a people robbed and plundered; all of them are snared in holes, and they are hidden in prison houses; they are for prey, and no one delivers; for plunder, and no one says, "Restore"* (Isaiah 42:22).

God enlightens us with dreams that give us the necessary wisdom to prosper even when others have been cheating us. God has conceived plans that empower us to create and access physical wealth in order to construct a successful life. God is always watching, so He sees when others cheat, abuse or deceive us. And He is able to restore to us what has been stolen and prosper us even more. Allow me illustrate by paraphrasing one particular account of Jacob:

> Laban had lied to Jacob and cheated him out of his wages ten different times. Jacob finally had enough. He planned to leave with his wives, his herd of livestock and all of his personal property. For Jacob and his family to remain working for Laban, a new agreement had to be made. All of the spotted and speckled livestock was to be culled from Laban's herds and given to Jacob as back payments to settle the gap of what was owed in unpaid wages. Laban went out and formed a separate flock (for Jacob) that consisted of all the male rams that were ringed and spotted, all the female goats that were speckled and spotted with white patches and all the black sheep. In that time period, goats with coats that bore these types of diverse markings were not considered desirable agriculture. Laban basically gathered up all the rejects and gave them to Jacob's sons. Jacob's sons were to take their new flock a three days' distance.

Meanwhile, Jacob was to stay and care for Laban's now solid flock.

God sent His angel to give Jacob a strategic dream that would cause him to create wealth and prosperity. Jacob shared the dream with his wives Leah and Rachel: "I had a dream at the time the flock conceived. I looked up and saw that the rams that mated with the she-goats were streaked, speckled and spotted. And the Angel of God said to me in the dream, 'Jacob.' And I said, 'Here IAM.' And He said, 'Look up and see, all the rams that mate with the flock are streaked, speckled and mottled; for I have seen all the deception and injustice that Laban has done to you.'"

When this was done, Jacob had a divine plan to prosper. He took fresh rods of poplar, almond and plane trees, and he peeled white streaks in them, exposing the white in the rods. Then Jacob set the rods, which he had peeled, where the flocks came inside to drink from the full watering troughs so that they floated around like a lamb or kid in the womb. And since they bred and conceived when they came to drink, the flocks bred and conceived what their eyes saw floating in the watery womb of the trough in the sight of the rods. Because that is what they had seen and imagined, the animals brought forth lambs and kids streaked, speckled and spotted.

Jacob separated the lambs, and, as he had done with the peeled rods, he also set the faces of the flocks toward the streaked and all the dark in the new flock of Laban. He put his own droves by themselves and did not let them breed with Laban's flock. Whenever the stronger animals were breeding, Jacob laid the rods in the watering troughs before the eyes of the flock so that they might see the spotted design and breed (conceive) among the rods. But whenever the feebler animals were breeding, Jacob omitted putting the rods before their sight so that the feebler animals would be Laban's and the stronger would be Jacob's. Thus, Jacob increased and became exceedingly rich. He had many sheep, goats, camels, donkeys, maidservants and menservants (see Genesis 30:37–43).

Like Jacob, God also gifts us with the power to harvest the vast, endless, eternal wealth that comes from His Spirit. God's divine knowledge, anointings and abilities are all resident within us! There is so much of the fullness of God dwelling within each of us that it will take all of eternity and beyond for us to discover, learn to receive and harvest all that our heavenly Father has freely given us. As Believers, our earthly bodies live and move in chronological time, while our spirit beings live in constant contact with eternity.

Ruth's Transition from Gleaner to Estate Owner

It is the Believer's responsibility to keep moving forward. Fear is always a present option that corrupts, so why choose a losing route when faith is always a winning choice that leads to eternal change. Decide fear has no power over you, then accomplish the impossible. Never hesitate to advance in the Kingdom of God as it advances—even if you have to press on in fear.

The landscapes of your internal being are ripe for harvest. Do not wait four more long months to glean. Instead, thrust in the sickle to gather prosperity and abundance from the affluence found in the center of the field. Take the keys (ownership) of the Kingdom, unlock the door (consciousness) of access and step into a fresh dimension of influence, taking on a new identity that will empower you to possess that broader mansion or prosperous state of being.

> *We are to fight from a position of victory to victory and to continually rejoice with thanksgiving in order to bring forth that same dimension of resurrection power that releases multiplication in our life.*

Never settle for sickness, disease, poverty or lack, living off of what was overlooked, discarded or left on the fringes or outskirts of the field. *Do you not say, "There are still four months and then comes the harvest." Behold, I say to you, lift up your eyes and look at the fields, for they are already white for harvest* (John 4:35)!

Ruth's youthful beauty, abiding love and loyalty empowered her to take on a courageous responsibility. Ruth had a gentle, yet decisive nature that embraced a difficult challenge. Her determined consistency healed her bitter mother-in-law Naomi. Ruth's faithful and humble perseverance achieved the impossible.

Ruth was once only a foreigner gleaning the fallen kernels of grain left in Boaz's fields by his servants. But by using her skillful imagination, her gifts and work ethics were noticed. Ruth saw an opportunity and imagined what was possible. Ruth knew if she applied herself and worked smart, there was an availability to become the owner of the field. Ruth pursued Boaz as her kinsman redeemer. She became his beautiful wife, the joint heir of his entire estate and the mother of the rich land proprietor Boaz's newborn son (see Ruth 4:1–13).

> *As Believers, our earthly bodies live and move in chronological time, while our spirit beings live in constant contact with eternity.*

The most mundane relationship can be changed for the better and become exciting by using the powers of a resourceful imagination. For the abundant life of prosperity to manifest, we must first accept it by faith. We simply choose to believe the life-giving, lavish visions that Christ is showing us.

When life gets tough, the righteous fall on their knees, and they ask God for His wisdom. When life knocks us down, we learn to humble ourselves, and God will lift us up again. When life shows us who we are, we can repent and change. When life shows us something ugly, we can close our eyes and pray. When we experience sadness, sorrow or grief, we can surrender our pain to God. He will restore our soul.

What will we choose to believe? True Believers believe they are Sons of God! *We are God's children in that He has raised us up in Jesus* (Acts 13:33).

Do you choose to believe that you are destined to be a rich, prosperous person of truth? Or do you choose to believe that you are a poor man, a beggar or, worse yet, a liar and a thief? *I will declare the decree: "The Lord has said to Me, 'You are My Son, today I have begotten You'"* (Psalm 2:7).

Let Us Pray

Dear Lord Jesus, thank you for giving me a new vision of Your supernatural strength arising from within my being. Empower me to tear down every mental stronghold. Remove my old thought patterns and outdated ways so that IAM able to conquer every physical and spiritual giant. Prepare me to be able to contain everything that You add to me. Empower me to support an increased measure of blessings until I can sustain the favor that comes with Your multiplication. Strengthen me to stand up under the weight of Your continual goodness.

Help me see and supply the needs of others. Give me the skills that are necessary to steward the resources You have entrusted to me. I ask for Your godly wisdom to prosper through the giving of tithes, alms and first fruit offerings. Empower me to adopt Your higher thoughts and glorious ways. Deliver me from being the borrower, gleaning from someone's leftovers. Help me to become the owner who has enough to lend and sow into every good work. Amen.

CHAPTER EIGHTEEN:

Overcoming Poverty and Lack

Mammon is a god that rules when we agree with the lack, the dis-ease and the poverty spirit. To be healed and for us to prosper, we have to break covenant with every form of poverty. Then as a result, we will also be delivered from our infirmities. To overcome poverty, disease and the love of money, we must form a covenant with God that places Him in the highest and first place in every area of our life. Covenant breaking robs God of the honor, tithe monies and blessings that are due Him. This calculated theft produces curses that reach back into our bloodlines to activate the damaging results of sin from four generations.

The unholy fruits of robbing God manifest in the lives of individuals as disease, emotional instability and mental difficulties. Individuals who have robbed God often experience physical theft, loss of properties and bankruptcy. Their relationships are plagued with betrayal, jealousy, adultery, immorality, impotence and perversion. They are either barren or experience the loss of their children through the murderous bloodshed of abortion, separation or divorce. They often exhibit a reprobate, twisted mind.

Those who possess a poor self-concept or are anxious or void of a strong work ethic will never get ahead in life. People who lack ambition blame their less than adequate environment on anything or anyone, but they never take any responsibility themselves. If they are employed, they blame their employer for paying them less than they deserve. Instead of putting forth a greater effort and doing more than is expected of them in order to earn a promotion, they slide along through life by doing as little as possible, and they often feel justified in cheating their boss of a good day's work. These types of untrustworthy individuals will not prosper in any of their ways because they do not operate in truth. People like this are continually deceived, and they are untruthful with others as a way of getting ahead.

Sadly, others consider their life's status to be limited due to their gender, race or his or her environmental circumstances. They are influenced by the superstition of believing in the chance star sign they were born under. Others attribute their negative circumstances to a lack of luck, simply a coincidence that took place from being in the wrong place at the wrong time. These are certainly not responsible views of reality.

Because he spends all of his mental energy worrying about everything, the poverty-stricken man remains plagued with lack. Where will he get his next meal, clean clothes to cover his body and a warm, safe place to lay his weary head? Who can he con, trick or threaten into giving him money? Will he need to beg, borrow or steal?

Personal Reflection Moment

1. Do you ever find yourself operating with a poverty mindset?
2. Do you ever make decisions based on a poverty mentality?
3. Consider what you worry about. Are you able to identify what may be hindering prosperity in your life?
4. Do you take honest responsibility for your reality?

The destitute man resents people of means and wealth, so his money flees away from him. His negative attitude about money prevents him from being able to draw money into his narrow circle. He greedily holds onto every penny he makes, never investing in anything including the betterment of himself. By repeating the same mental exercises of doubt, fearing to hope because of an expectation of disappointment or living in unbelief, the spirit of poverty takes root. This pattern of downward struggles and misfortune is full of destructive thoughts. These harmful, self-defeating emotional patterns will continue to dig their way deeper and deeper into the depths of despair. The fruits that are grown and developed are failure, lack, depression and disease.

Avoid pessimistic, fear-based people; they draw poverty and lack into their small circle or sphere of very limited, narrow influence. Poverty kills creativity; it places strict limitations on one's mind by hedging in or even destroying the positive use of his or her imagination. The person who possesses a poverty mentality will remain in a state of poverty, even if he or she is given millions of dollars. *Will you set your eyes on that which is not? For riches certainly make themselves wings; they fly away like an eagle toward heaven* (Proverbs 23:5).

A poverty mentality destroys ambition. Poverty rejects the hope that things will ever change, leaving the person a slave to their own indebtedness. Debt is like quicksand; it draws you in deeper and deeper until you are stuck, submerged in muck and up to your neck in bills and with bill collectors. Debt then slowly strangles the life out and takes you completely under. To prevent debt, tithe to God and make a habit of saving a percentage of your income from every paycheck. Learn to make a budget, and save up for purchases instead of using credit cards. Then pay off your credit card balances every month instead of paying high interest rates on partial payments. Safely invest your money to overcome lack, poverty and indebtedness.

> *To be healed and for us to prosper, we have to break covenant with every form of poverty.*

Negative, critical, judgmental thoughts, words and deeds create an ugly, negative world full of hatred, war and prejudice, which cause poverty and disease. People who maintain a habitual victim thought process always produce a poverty mentality of consistent lack. Their character is locked into the lie that life has dealt them a losing set of cards, while others always get a straight flush to win every hand.

When we stop being the victim, repent of blaming others for our condition and stop robbing God, we will arise to a new level of brilliance. Then our light will shine as a beckon out of darkness. Moral, principled and honorable thoughts empower people to discover their hidden gifts, talents and God-given strengths. Old habits die hard, so they must be renounced, repented of and replaced by positive thoughts, actions and a productive inner belief system.

> *That we should no longer be children, tossed back and forth being carried about with every wind of doctrine, by the trickery of men, in the cunning craftiness of deceitful plotting, but, speaking the truth in love, may grow up in all things into Him who is the head—Christ* (Ephesians 4:14–15).

When we repent, we are able to change our internal voice. Instead of growing old, we are able to experience life to its fullest by living large and maturing gracefully. Live a healthy, well-balanced life of peace and harmony that is spiritually blessed, mentally sound and physically fit. Then you will overcome poverty, lack and all sickness and disease.

Renewing of the mind with the Word of God changes the way we think and respond to things. Repentance enables us to leave our past history behind. Higher thoughts and verbal expressions empower us to apprehend a new way of life; therefore, our destiny changes.

Our greatest enemies are apathy, self-pity, poverty, fear and discord, ignorance and illiteracy. Learn how to prosper over every form of lack, and destroy the influences of poverty. Repentance brings deliverance from all of these curses, infirmities, diseases and afflictions. Pray that God's great grace will give you a new restorative vision that opens up amazing opportunities and new territories for you to possess. Moving into prosperity requires the renewing of your mind by the washing of the Word of God, an increase of angelic action and divine interventions, which tear down the walls of incredible opposition.

The private war with carnal thoughts that we wage within our mind and the level of victory we gain determines the anointings, degree of authority and the amount of favor we carry in order to influence the Church, society and governmental structures. To break off a poverty mindset, we must think success and prosperity. A healthy thought life will empower us to sow life-giving, creative seeds into good ground that produce new ideas for income streams. Creative ideas empower people to gain resources that cause great increase and abundance so that they have the ability to meet every need. Learn to bless your increase with thanksgiving; do not curse it with grumbling or complaining. God rewards the thankful heart.

When I was raising money for my mission crusade to India, my dear friends donated $3,000 toward my trip. Shortly after I received their check, I called and thanked them for the large sum of money. I let the couple know how much their giving blessed me and that it had paid for over half of my trip! I thanked God for my generous friends. Within minutes, Stephen and his beautiful wife, Rosalba, called back. God had spoken to their loving hearts; they decided to double their donation, and they offered to pay for the whole trip. During the week I spent in India, I witnessed thirty-eight thousand people receive Jesus as their Savior for the first time. Multiplied thousands experienced miracles, healing and deliverance. Stephen and Rosalba's money was well-invested in souls for all eternity.

God's solution to poverty is always multiplication. Poverty, infirmity and false religion are a threefold cord of abuse. A threefold cord is nothing when compared to the all-powerful Trinity. It is time to agree with God and set yourself and all of the captives free. Renew your mind with the Word of God, and divorce small thinking. Dismantle a religious spirit, and come out from under the spirit of poverty.

The condition of a person's soul cannot be determined by the outer workings of his or her life alone. Everyone has both honorable and dishonorable thoughts that allow them to reap both good and evil. A good seed cannot produce evil, and an evil seed can never produce anything good. Jesus called the Pharisees a brood of snakes! How can evil men like you speak what is good and right? *The full abundance that is found in a man's heart determines the words of his speech and his words determine his actions* (Matthew 12:34).

> *Moral, principled and honorable thoughts empower people to discover their hidden gifts, talents and God-given strengths.*

We would like to believe that we suffer just because we are pure and holy. The reality is we often bring suffering on ourselves by the evil thoughts, bitter stains, anger or unforgiving intentions of the heart. Wisdom teaches us that as we look back on the sufferings in our life, we will discover the underlying toxic thoughts. We will recognize the immoral or selfish actions that produced our ignorant, blind or deaf state.

Center yourself in Christ. Then concentrate your focus upon developing a plan to perfect one thing in your life at a time. Daily pray, decree and declare, "I am always improving. Today and every day I am becoming more successful and Christlike in every way!" The negative thoughts you think and the destructive words you say will condemn you to a life of misery, pain, loneliness and poverty. Nourish and protect your life dreams; for if they fall to the ground for others to trample, they will be devoured and die like a bird with a crippled wing that can't take flight. Positive, creative, hope-filled words empower you to imagine how to achieve the impossible dream.

Let Us Pray

Dear Lord Jesus, thank you for delivering me from all curses of mental instability, infirmity and emotional and physical sickness and disease. Thank you for delivering me from all curses of theft, bankruptcy, poverty and every form of lack. I repent of being a covenant-breaker, and I repent of not honoring You in all the areas of my life. Please forgive me and my bloodline back to four generations for robbing You of tithes and offerings. Renew my mind by the washing of Your holy Word, and remove all negative, critical and judgmental thoughts, words and deeds. Help me to slay my internal enemies of apathy, self-pity, fear, discord, ignorance and illiteracy. Amen.

CHAPTER NINETEEN

Restored to Sonship

The Sons of God are the Believers who have taken their place inside the Father's heart. The Sons of God have mastered the principle of dwelling in the power of the end result. This is what makes the Believer in Jesus Christ an unstoppable force. *Son, you are always with Me by My side, and all that I have is already yours* (Luke 15:31). When we dwell with the Father in His mansions, we are joint heirs with Christ. We abide in God, so we have full access to all of Him.

We all have acted like one of the two give me prodigal sons when we first started our spiritual journey. There are gradient phases we must master in order to develop spiritual maturity. Each of us must progressively move from the *give me* stage to the *use and utilize me* syndrome. When we ask God to use us, it often really means that we want to be in the limelight so that others can see how great and wonderful we are. The next phase in the maturation process is called the *make me* stage. This is where we learn how to develop a servant's attitude so that we will be concerned for others, not just for ourselves. And finally, we reach the *search me* stage (attitude). We ask the Lord to look within the closets of our hearts to see if there is still any sin, evil ways, fears, disease or strongholds of corrupt thought left within. A destructive mental stronghold is an argument that you believe and hold to that contradicts the person and power of Christ.

To become the Sons (and Daughters) of God, we must mature in our thinking and actions as I have noted above. This spiritual maturation process is depicted in the biblical story of the prodigal son. Allow me to paraphrase Luke 15:11–32:

> The younger of the two sons inappropriately said to his father, "Father, *give me* (stage one) the share of the property that falls to me." So the Father divided the estate between his two (give me) sons.
>
> The younger son gathered all of his belongings, and he traveled to a distant country. There, he wasted his fortune. In his loneliness, he held lavish, wild parties. He gave gifts to be seen and admired by men in order to feel important and to gain companions. He foolishly spent everything he had on reckless, immoral living.
>
> A severe famine occurred. He did without and was in great need. In desperation, he forced himself on a citizen who sent him out into the fields to feed pigs. He would have gladly eaten the pigs' slop, but it could not satisfy his hunger, and no one was giving him anything. When his senses finally came back into his right mind, he said, "How many of my father's hired men have more than enough food, while I am dying here of hunger!" I will get up and go to my father, and I will say to him, "Father, I have sinned (stage four; repentance) against heaven and in your sight. I am no longer worthy to be called your son. Therefore, *make me* (stage two) a servant like your hired men."
>
> So the prodigal got up and came to his father. In his heart, he said, "Search me (stage three), O God, and know my heart; try me, and know my anxieties; and see if there is any wicked way in me, and lead me in the way everlasting" (Psalm 139:23–24).
>
> But while he was still a long way off, his father saw him, was moved with compassion for him and ran to embrace him with a kiss. And the son said to him, "Father, I have sinned (stage four; repentance) against heaven and in your sight; I am no longer worthy to be called your son make me a servant."

But the father replied (stage five; forgiveness), "As for you, my (prodigal) son, know the God of your father, and serve Him with a loyal heart and with a willing mind; for the Lord searches all hearts and understands all the intent of the thoughts. If you seek Him, He will be found by you; but if you forsake Him, He will cast you off forever" (1 Chronicles 28:9).

Then the Father commanded his servants (stage six; restoration), "Quickly! Bring out the best robe for the guest of honor, and put it on my son. Give him My covenant ring for his hand and clean sandals for his feet. Bring the fattened calf, and slaughter it, and let us invite everyone to feast and celebrate. For this prodigal son of mine was as good as dead and is alive again; he was lost and has been found." So they began to celebrate.

Now his older son was in the field. When he returned and approached the house, he heard music and dancing. So he summoned one of the servants and began asking what was meant by this celebration. And the servant said to him, "Your brother has come, and your father has killed the fattened calf because he has received him back safe and sound."

But the elder brother became angry and deeply resentful, and he was not willing to go in; so his father came out and began pleading with him. But he said to his father, "Look! These many years I have served you, and I have never neglected or disobeyed your command. Yet you have never *given me* so much as a young goat so that I might celebrate with my friends. But when this other son of yours arrived, who has devoured your estate with immoral women, you slaughtered that fattened calf for him!"

The father said to him, "Son, you are always with me, and all that is mine is yours. But it was fitting to celebrate and rejoice, for this brother of yours was as good as dead and has begun to live. He was lost and has been found."

The people you have faithfully loved, served and invested in, but you have not seen your returned harvest from their selfish, *give me* prodigal lifestyle yet, shall repent of their *use me* attitudes. They shall break free of their self-centered, *make me* bondages, and they shall produce an abundant life as they invite God to search them and know them.

The prodigals will enter back into their right mind, come home, be restored and turn back to the ways of God in order to fulfill their unique destiny. No matter what these once prodigal sons or daughters did, their finally being in their right mind will give them a newly found confidence in the Father's faithful love and goodness. The total acceptance of the dissolute, immoral, degenerate prodigals into the beloved family of God caused the previously uncontrolled prodigal to gain his own self-control. Forgiveness caused the immoral, self-indulgent, *give me* prodigal to forge his way through every depravity and perceived limitation.

> *We must all awaken back into our right minds to realize our desperate need of being saved from ourselves, sin and disease.*

Each of us has knowingly been the dissipated prodigal at some point or another. We have each chosen to fall far short of a goal by not using the full measure of the knowledge of the glorious abilities that we have been given access to. Instead of receiving all that the Father has planned and reserved for us to inherit as joint heirs of Christ, we have compromised and settled for a life that is reckless, wasteful and is void of power.

Personal Reflection Moment

We must ask ourselves the hard questions in order to know where we stand in our spiritual maturity when push comes to shove.

1. Do you, as a Believer in the Christ, carry within you enough love, faith and moral fiber to influence others as well as yourself?
2. Can you impact just one other person, or can you touch dozens, hundreds, thousands or even favorably inspire the whole of society? Or have you joined the world with their wicked deeds and violent actions, so

there is no difference or evident demarcation line between the Sons of God and the sons of this worldly domain?

3. Instead of seeking the Father's loving face, have you squandered your gifts, talents and abilities by spending your time on worldly pleasures? Or have you wasted valuable time (for example, watching TV) on mindless entertainment?

4. Do all of your energies revolve around your own comforts and selfish, worldly pursuits?

We must all awaken back into our right minds to realize our desperate need of being saved from ourselves, sin and disease. Though hopeless of ever becoming all we were destined to become, we know that anything would be better than our current situation of wallowing in a sin-filled, miry pit of filth and worldly debauchery. Remembering our righteous state as the beloved Father's son or daughter provokes us to cry out for the Father's mercy, knowing that it is only by His grace that we will be saved, healed and restored.

People will forget what you have said, and they may also forget what you have accomplished, but they will never forget how you have treated them, especially if you have showered them with love, honor, kindness and respect. If you want a good return on your investment, always influence people with mercy, grace and lovingkindness.

Our heavenly Father daily looks for us to lift our face heavenward. God the Father diligently watches, patiently waits and listens for our faint, repentant cry that asks Him for deliverance. While we are still addicted, ensnared in sexual perversions or paralyzed by fear, while we are still adulterers, fornicators or self-centered abortionists (the list goes on), our heavenly Father comes and extends His loving hands to pull us out of the snare of sin. He draws our twisted, infirmed bodies to His chest. With one touch of the Master's hand, we are cleansed, forgiven, healed, delivered, set free and restored to our righteous position as a beloved son or daughter. We are made whole again.

When the prodigal son returned to his right mind and went through a spiritual transformation, he was able to escape the filth of the worldly pigpen. Our returning to the Father's house (divine mansions) empowers us to be restored to our covenant place as Sons of God. The Father patiently watches and waits for our appearing. When we repent and return to our right mind, the Father lovingly clothes us in robes of righteousness. Righteousness repositions us in a place of grace and right standing so that we can start thinking the higher thoughts of God.

When the filth, dirt and mire are washed off our hands, they are clean again. The covenanted signet ring is placed on our finger. When we are restored as Sons of God, we can ascend into heavenly places to function in the ways of God's wisdom. When we feast upon the meat of the Word, we become pure of heart. This level of spiritual maturity and understanding empowers us to take on the image and likeness of God.

The past cannot dictate our tomorrows if we believe that God has already freed us from the old man's habitual ways. We are crucified with Christ; nevertheless, we also live in Him having been resurrected into a new life form. *I have been crucified with Christ; it is no longer I who live, but Christ lives in me; and the life which I now live in the flesh I live by faith in the Son of God, who loved me and gave Himself for me* (Galatians 2:20).

The past cannot dictate our tomorrows if we believe that God has already freed us from the old man's habitual ways.

As a new creature in Christ, we are confident that God will complete in us what He has begun. By dwelling with the end results in focus and presently assuming that identity, we will finally realize the vision of what God desires for us to become as fact.

To be born again means that we become conscious of leaving our sinful, natural state of limitations behind to rise to a higher place in the Spirit. *Being confident of this very thing, that He who has begun a good work in you will complete it until the day of Jesus Christ* (Philippians 1:6). When we are born again, we become Sons of God and joint heirs with Christ. All of heaven's angels, wealth, glory and powerful resources are at our disposal.

The faith that we exercised when we prayed the prayer of salvation completely changed our spirit, soul and body. Prayer rearranges and enlarges the earthly vessel that we dwell in so that our body becomes the castle for our King Jesus, the host for the Kingdom of God and His Holy Spirit. *If you ask anything in My name, I will do it* (John 14:14).

This does not mean that we speak the numerous names of God as if they are some magical mantra. As Believers, we take on the spiritual nature, supremacy and attributes of that distinct name of God. *Because he set his love on Me, therefore I will save him; I will set him* (securely) *on high, because he knows My name* (confidently trusts that I will never abandon him) (Psalm 91:14). We do this by applying God's knowledge and adapting to the understanding of the creative power that is found in that particular function of God's name.

> *You did not choose Me, but I chose you and appointed you that you should go and bear fruit, and that your fruit should remain, that whatever you ask the Father in My name* (nature, authority, character, image and likeness) *He may give you* (John 15:16).

When we consciously reflect or project the image, influence, trait or nature of Jesus, we rise to take on the attributes of His sonship. As heirs of God, we have access to all the wisdom, power, joys and pleasures the Father has to offer. *Happy is the man who finds wisdom, and the man who gains understanding* (Proverbs 3:13). When we are renewed in the power of our mind, we cast off our mire-caked sandals of sin, and we receive the healing transforming shoes of the gospel of salvation and peace.

God is love. He is not critical, judgmental or condemning. If our concept of God is one of a cruel taskmaster who punishes (which produces fear and negative thoughts), we can be sure that we have adapted a lie. We have embraced a false belief system about our loving heavenly Father. By allowing our mind to wander from the higher thoughts and ways of God, we, like the prodigal, fall away from the Father's house to create our own misery.

When we abandon God, we decide to live in the pigpen of sin, consciously focused on our lack and poverty. We have intentionally squandered our spiritual wealth by willfully adopting earthly, sensual ways. While we are knowingly practicing sin, we no longer have the confidence to approach God with boldness in order to prosper and be in good health. The soul becomes bound by the accusations of shame and guilt. Like the prodigal, we end up deliberately eating the pig's dirty slop and wallowing in the mire of disease and poverty with all the other filthy swine.

Repentance and the shed blood of Jesus have the power to cleanse, restore and renew us back into our right mind. We can once again connect to the love of the Father, the mind of Christ. Repentance cancels the regrets of the past. It cleans the slate of wrongs to give us a brand new start in order to produce a brilliant future.

Our heavenly Father came to us in our sin, redeemed and forgave us and placed His covenant ring of inheritance on our finger, which restores us to a royal sonship. All of heaven rejoices when one person repents at salvation. The fatted calf is brought in so that we can enjoy a feast of celebration with our friends and family. Our Father cloaks us in the finest robe of righteousness. God extends the eternal life of favor to us. We are given the grace to obtain wealth, health and prosperity. *There is therefore now no condemnation to those who are in Christ Jesus, who do not walk according to the flesh, but according to the Spirit* (Romans 8:1).

There is nothing that we can do in our own strength to earn sonship. It is the gift of grace through the Spirit of Christ that raises us up and back into a position of sonship so that we can regain our inheritance. *For it is the Father's good pleasure to give us the Kingdom. And he said to him, "Son, you are always with me, and all that I have is yours"* (Luke 15:31).

Let's Pray

Dear Lord Jesus, You are the firstborn, the one and only beloved Son of God. It is through Your precious blood and stripes that I am saved, healed and delivered. Thank you for being the door that gives me entrance into the Father's heart to become a true Son of God and joint heir with Christ. Thank You for cleansing me of all my sins so that I can return to my Father's house and live in the mansion You have gone before me to prepare. As I repent, You return me to my right mind, so I am able to apprehend the mind of Christ. Now that I have been saved from my sin, born again and crucified with Christ, it is no longer I who live, but now I invite You, Christ Jesus, to live in and through me. Amen.

Author's Note

In the succeeding volume of the *IMAGINE* series, we will bring full circle all the concepts learned previously in each of the volumes. You will discover the keys to successfully maintain your new identity in Christ, and you will gain deeper revelation regarding God's creative power, divine desire, imaginative dreams, godly disciplines of the imagination and fruitful growth. Volume V delivers sound biblical teachings of how to use your creative imagination to release, prophesy into your God-ordained destiny and the destinies of nations. Get ready to acquire the necessary knowledge and wisdom to effectively operate, persevere and prosper as a true Son of God and as One New Man.

About the Author

DR. BARBIE L. BREATHITT

DR. BARBIE BREATHITT is a certified prophetic life coach (AskBarbie.com), published best-selling author, dedicated educator and experienced revelatory teacher of the divine, supernatural manifestations of God, whose greatest desire is to see other reach, fullfill and enjoy their destiny in God. She is recognized around the world as a leading master dream analyst (DreamsDecoder.com) and healing evangelist with deliverance, signs, wonders and creative miracles following. Barbie's prophetic seer gifting and deep spiritual insights have helped and equipped thousands of people, including business, media and government leaders, and ministries in over 40 nations understand God's mystical ways.

Dr. Barbie Breathitt teaches individuals, trains corporate professionals and business teams, government leaders and churches how to recognize, respond to and release the activity of God with unique strategies. Her sincere pursuit of God's Kingdom and His eternal truth make Barbie's Texas-based Breath of the Spirit Ministries, Inc. a predominant worldwide foundation.

An experienced teacher, published author, prophetic voice, dream analyst and healing evangelist, she has released God's love, presence and breath in prisons, hospitals, streets, Europe, third-world nations, television, radio and the internet. Her deepest desire is to see people fulfill their unique destiny here on earth. Barbie's training, resources and personal ministry help others to interpret and apply the direction God gives them through encounters, dreams and visions.

Barbie Breathitt personally learned and now passionately teaches God's Love, Presence and Breath. Her astute prophetic voice and accurate dream analyses have blessed those in prisons, hospitals, Europe and third-world nations, enabling many hungry people to grow. Barbie has abandoned herself to the Holy Spirit with miracles, signs and wonders following. Many individuals have been miraculously healed in her meetings while others have experienced the Presence of the Spirit as never before. Her infectious humor promotes unity with those inside and outside the church walls.

An ordained healing evangelist, Barbie has ministered for over thirty-five years around the world. Barbie established and conducted three prophetic training centers. Barbie now lives in Texas and opened Breath of the Spirit Center of Training in 2004. Breath of the Spirit offers a variety of courses on Healing, Revelatory Gifts, Dream Interpretation and Evangelistic Outreaches.

SPEAKING ENGAGEMENTS

Traveling around the world to share wisdom and insights regarding sound, biblical dream interpretation, Barbie is available for conferences, teaching and hands-on training. Please contact Barbie's ministry at Breath of the Spirit Ministries, Inc. through email (info@DreamsDecoder.com), the website (DreamsDecoder.com) or by phone at (972) 253-6653 for more information.

The *IMAGINE* Series

Volume I will help you understand and fully comprehend that the Spirit of Christ dwells mightily within your sanctified imagination. Discover how to supplant the carnal mindset that has limited God and the displaying of His grandeur in your life. By resting in and experiencing the presence and glory of God, you will be empowered to receive and harness His truth, divine wisdom, revelation and supernatural faith to confidently realize, embrace and achieve your unique purpose and grand destiny in this new era!

God has given you a riveting new identity in this new era! Volume II inspires and imparts how to further unlock and mature your imagination to fulfill God's purposes for your life. Discover what it is and how to shed your worldly, carnal self—how to transition into your higher IAM state of being in Christ. Advance beyond the limitations of the third dimension, and gain supernatural knowledge of the mysterious workings of the unrestrictive, four-dimensional realm of the Spirit.

The marvelous design and divine workings of the inspired imagination is further unveiled in this third volume. You will gain applicable spiritual understanding of how to access, unlock and interpret the meanings of visions and dreams that God skillfully fashions within your imagination. You will discover how to access your God-given authority. You will unite with the Fire of God to believe, see and prophesy in the NOW realm of God's faith. Through a broadened understanding of God's Word and clear spiritual insights into the profound power of imaginative prayer, you will be able to access the answers to your prayers that have been waiting on you to discover from the Genesis of creation. *IMAGINE* Volume III will equip and fully transition you into your new and glory-purposed identity in Christ. Your faith in God will explode into the supernatural faith of God!

In this instructive and illuminating volume, you will gain divine knowledge about the healing power of the subconscious, God's imaginative power and creative miracles. Volume IV will challenge what you believe, see and reason as truth and will help you identify the hindrances to having your prayers answered. God is restoring His people as One New Man! By using your sanctified imagination, you will discover how to come into agreement with God in order to effectively release your prophetic voice in this new era. You will obtain valuable instruction on how to increase, advance and prosper for God's kingdom purposes.

This fifth volume of the *IMAGINE* series brings the concepts learned in previous volumes full circle. Now that you have believed, beheld and obtained your new identity, you will discover the keys to successfully maintain that identity. You will encounter God's creative power, divine desire, godly disciplines of the imagination and lasting growth. The time to advance is NOW! Volume V delivers sound biblical teachings of how to use your creative imagination to release and prophesy into your God-ordained destiny and the destinies of nations. You will acquire the necessary knowledge and wisdom to effectively operate, persevere and prosper as a true Son of God and as One New Man.

DecodeMyDream.com

ONLINE DREAM JOURNAL

Barbie Breathitt is excited that so many people in God's Kingdom are exploring the understanding of dreams. Barbie's 30 years of study and experience in biblically-based, spirit-led dream interpretation are available in an online learning experience.

DreamsDecoder.com and DecodeMyDream.com are our interactive web sites, impacting dreamers all over the world. We believe it is vitally important to record God-given dreams and to search out the messages they contain. The site provides a free online dream journal, dream evaluations, dream mapping, prophetic analysis and comprehensive dream certification training.

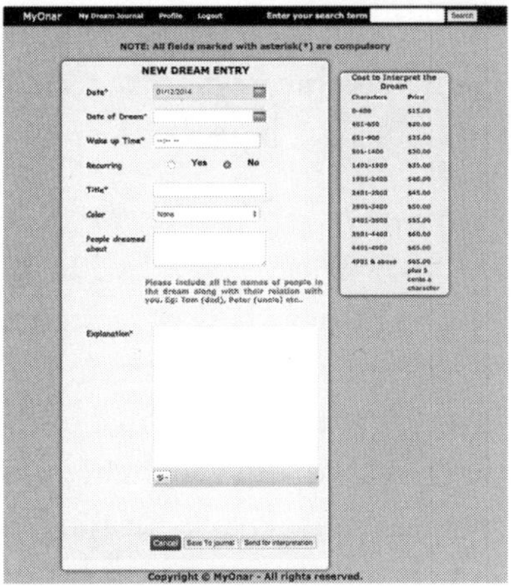

Sign up for your free online dream journal at DreamsDecoder.com. From the dream journal, you can easily submit your dreams for analysis by Barbie and our highly skilled dream analysts.

For additional resources by Dr. Barbie L. Breathitt, please visit
DreamsDecoder.com
Breath of the Spirit Ministries, Inc.
PO Box 1356 | Lake Dallas, TX 75065
(972) 253-6653

BOOKS

Dream Encounters–Seeing Your Destiny from God's Perspective is the "Rosetta Stone" to interpreting the illusive vapors of dreams. Uniquely inspired, and written to convince the greatest skeptics, and educate the most ardent believer, "Dream Encounters" will bring God's perspective, and understanding to the symbolic, visual, love letters, in the mysterious world of dreams. Take a journey into the sub–conscious night parables of the soul, to learn how dream truths impact your world; give direction, purpose, and destiny. Gain valuable keys to success by unlocking the mysteries of your dreams. Available as a paperback book, digital book or audio book.

Gateway to the Seer Realm: Look Again to See Beyond the Natural is written by Dr. Barbie Breathitt a gifted Seer who has years of personal experience interpreting dreams and ministering in the prophetic realm. You will gain valuable insights into understanding the ways of God and the divine supernatural realms of vision, dreams, angels, healing and destiny. Open new dimensions of revelation knowledge to learn how to access the Seer realm through intimate daily communication with God.

Dream Seer: Searching for the Face of the Invisible is written by Dr. Barbie L. Breathitt to help the reader understand the Seer Realms of angels, divine visions, the voice and presence of the Lord and dimensions where the ethereal vapors of our dreams will become substantial presences when we believe that anything is possible with God. God is the giver of dreams. Jesus is also the Redeemer. So, like a knight in shining armor, He comes to restore the dreams we have allowed to fall by the wayside. The Holy Spirit inspires us to recall the images He sent long ago. God has mapped out our future. He brings the events of the world to bear on our individual circumstances as He wills. When the events of our lives coincide with the correct timing of His plans, the next phase of our destiny ensues. The Holy Spirit knows the perfect time to bring the dreams and plans He has formulated to enable our purpose to come to pass.

There is only one right interpretation, God's. Every thing else is only shades of gray. Dream Interpreter will give you skill to correctly decipher the symbolism of your dreams. *Dream Interpreter* decodes symbols, types and shadows of images from a heavenly perspective in order to reveal the hidden mysteries that are contained within. Dream Interpreter will help the reader translate spiritual perceptions and happenings to accurately discern the events of the night. The gifted dream interpreter can decipher, convert and transform a concealed secret and then develop a blueprint for prosperity. You can learn to understand the evolution of vivid visions and dreams, the graphic picture language of nightmares and night terrors that come to visit and present truth about one's life. As a wise counsellor or life coach, dream interpreters fashion destiny bubbling up from the depths of the person's soul-potential to successfully guide the dreamer.

Acquiring a working knowledge of dream symbolism will enhance your ability to decipher the profound meanings of each symbol and then unlock the interpretation of every one of your dreams. Knowledge is power so learn to understand the mysteries that are hidden in your dreams. Their divine secrets will release your concealed potential so that you can design the destiny you have always longed for. Access the revelation knowledge stored in the pages of *A to Z Dream Symbology Dictionary*. Glean from ten thousand keywords and symbolic meanings that will inspire you to delve deeper into understanding why a certain animal, object, person, place, vehicle, article of clothing, tool, home, food, flower, weather pattern, action, emotion, color, or number appeared in your subconscious dream.

In her book, *Angels in God's Kingdom*, Dr. Barbie L. Breathitt propels readers beyond a natural understanding of the world around them to perceive and navigate the divine supernatural realms of the invisible world of angels. This one-of-a-kind comprehensive Biblical resource is full of progressive revelation and inspired spiritual truths. Dr. Barbie L. Breathitt covers fascinating topics detailing the origin, existence, and abode of angelic beings, their names, ministry functions, duties, and little known facts about the classifications of angels. She explores the nature of angels, the bold power of active faith and how the anointings of angels, seraphim, cherubim, heavenly creatures and host connect and guide us to and through the spirit world. Barbie shares her real life angelic encounters and the knowledge she has received through her diverse visitations, as well as her traumatic experience with the spirit of death. Discover the mystery of how recognizing the presence of powerful angels can redeem time when they are invited to step out of eternity to assist us in miracles, healing and deliverance. Learn how to prosper as the angels in God's Kingdom collide with the lawless evil forces of darkness and destruction. Gain spiritual understanding of how God's holy, intelligent angels clash with Satan's demons and diabolical fallen angels in today's modern world. Discover how the giants from the days of Noah are currently affecting society. And how we can defeat them through the blood of Jesus.

When Will My Dreams Come True? This handy booklet provides valuable detailed descriptions on dreams, visions and spiritual encounters. The information shared in these pages will educate the dreamer on the biblical techniques of dream interpretation. Through the study and application of the Hebrew alphabet and numbers, you will develop an Issachar anointing to discern the days, times and seasons of your dreams coming to pass. This collection of data research, priceless dream interpretation nuggets, gradient echelons of revelation, and prophetic vocabulary and terminology assembled in these pages will instruct dreamers on how to record and accurately interpret the meaning of their dreams, so they can pray, decree and declare them into being.

DREAM SYMBOL CARDS

These artistically designed dream symbol cards enable the dreamer to tap into the hidden meanings of the symbols that appear in many dreams and visions. These cards are also useful in helping the believer decipher the symbolic language that God uses to communicate through the revelatory realm of the Spirit. "God is speaking powerfully through dreams in this hour. So many believers are having significant dreams but do not always understand the significance of the symbols within them. Barbie Breathitt has done a marvellous job of preparing dream cards as a tremendous tool to help this process. They are very high quality and fully laminated for long-term use. I was impressed when I saw them." Patricia King XP Ministries (xpministries.com).

Acquire all of Barbie's artistically designed, laminated Dream Encounter Symbols Cards. They are available as single dream cards, in an excel spreadsheet or in spiral-bound collections.

Dream Encounters Symbols Volume I features the original 23 dream cards starter set with 1433 unique symbol definitions which makes an excellent gift for those who have a desire to learn the meanings of their dreams. The collection includes Animals, Apparel & Clothing, Body Parts, Color, Color and Music Healing, Creatures Great, Creatures Small, God's Dream Language, Going Places, Going More Places, Home Furnishings, Jewels, Musical Instruments, Numbers, People, Seers' Word of Knowledge Ministry Card, Spiritual, More Spiritual, Tools, U. S. State, Vehicles, and Weather and Natural Elements.

Dream Encounters Symbols Volume II has 18 different dream cards with 619 different symbol definitions. The collection includes Birds (4 dream symbol cards containing a myriad of positive and negative winged creatures), Bugs and Insects (3 cards), Money and Finance, Nutrition (5 cards outlining the meaning of different foods, sweets, meats and vegetables), Plants and Flowers (4 cards detail what different floral arrangements and bouquets represent. God is giving His Bride flowers in her dream. What is He saying to you?), and Varied contains a list of Frequent Dream Symbols.

Dream Encounters Symbols Volume III has an additional 29 spiral bound dream cards that combines 913 symbols complied in helpful categories for ease of study and use. The collection includes, Body Parts (an extensive compilation of 5 dream symbol cards), Building, Rooms & Structures (4 cards), People (12 individual cards listing careers, professions and callings), Spiritual & Military Weapons of War (4 dream symbol cards describing the spiritual weapons of prayer available to believers), and Vehicles (4 dream symbol cards boats, ships, trucks, cars, vans, airplanes, rockets and more).

Action Symbols Volume IV, has 13 artistically designed spiral bound dream symbol cards with 386 different movements such as flying, running, transporting, and translating actions.

Dream Sexology has 4 unique and informative dream symbol cards with 95 unique symbol definitions that explain the meanings of your intimate naked dream language.

Sports & Recreation Dream Symbols contains 13 dream symbol cards full of 321 different hobbies, sports, games and much more to help you take an active part in the game of life instead of sitting on the sidelines observing the excitement of others.

TEACHING SERIES

The Dream Encounter MP3 Downloads and Manual is designed to teach, train, activate, and impart the skills to interpret and understand how God communicates to us through dreams and visions of the night. Jesus continues to teach through night parables, in other words, inspired dreams. The Bible gives us three keys that will be used in the end-time revival and outpouring of the Holy Spirit. The course topics include: Dreams, Visions, Transportations, Translations, Lucid Dreams, Colors, Numbers, Dream Symbols, Dream Interpretation, and Dream Teams and Outreaches.

The Revelatory Encounter MP3 Downloads and Manual is a prophetic course designed to teach, train, activate, and impart the ability to hear God's voice for yourself and others. This training helps you recognize and remove hindrances to hearing God's still, small voice. The course topics include: Developing Godly Character and Integrity, Old and New Testament Prophets, False Prophets, Immature Prophets, God's Friends, Knowing God's Voice, Difference between the Gift of Prophecy and the Prophetic Office, Forms of Revelation, Four Categories of Prophecy, Spirit of Prophecy, Nine Gifts of the Holy Spirit, Interpretation, Application, The Seer, The Watchmen, Intercession, Prayer, Intimacy, Spiritual Authority, and Developing Prophetic Ministry Teams.

The Angelic Encounter MP3 downloads and Manual is a course that establishes a biblical foundation for the proof and ministry of angels. Topics include: What are Angels? Ministry of Angels; Types, Functions, and Characteristics of Angels; Satan and Fallen Angels; and Angels and the Death of the Saints. Barbie shares personal experiences of angelic visitations from her life.

The Healing Encounter MP3 Downloads and Manual is designed to teach, train, activate and impart the belief, skills and abilities to move in the healing ministry. Topics include: Introduction to Healing; Jesus, the Healer; Issues of the Heart; Four Aspects of Healing; The Faith Realm; Take Your Authority; You Get What You Expect; Miracles Today; Hindrances to Miracles; Suffering in Regards to Healing; God's Voice of Healing; You Must See it to Be it!; Keep Your Healing; Healing Scriptures; Baptism with the Holy Spirit; and Walking in the Healing Ministry.

OTHER RESOURCES

The Hand Prayer Points Chart is a reference card that matches illnesses and diseases with prayer points on the hand. Great for intercessors who need clear direction for their prayers.

The Foot Prayer Points Chart is a reference card that matches the organs of the body, illnesses and diseases with prayer points on the foot. Great for intercessors who need clear direction for their prayers.

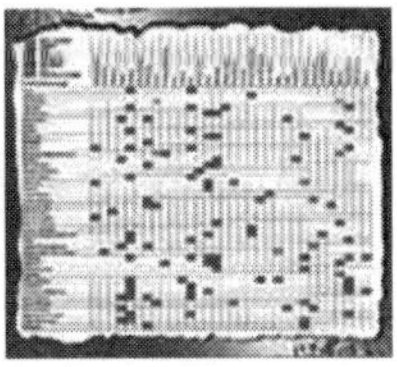

Healing Card is a reference card that matches illnesses and diseases with possible spiritual root causes. This Healing card is birthed from Barbie's ministry experiences and encounters of seasoned intercessors and those in healing ministries. Great for intercessors and individuals who need clear direction for their healing prayers.

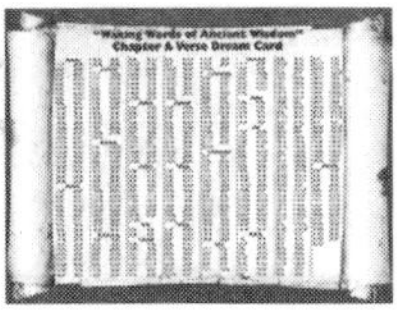

Waking Words of Ancient Wisdom Make it a practice to notice the time on the digital clock as you awaken from a spiritually significant dream. The numbers displayed on the digital clock are often keys to help understand the message God is giving you in your dreams. Note the time on your clock, then look up the corresponding chapter and verse in the Bible. Allow the Holy Spirit to quicken the intended "Waking Words of Ancient Wisdom" to your heart and apply them in your life. This is a wonderful way to daily explore the Bible while you seek the deeper meanings of the treasures God is revealing to you through your dreams. Visit BarbieBreathitt.com to obtain detailed directions for use.

Dream Encounter Anointing Oil: Anoint yourself every night with this fragrant dream enhancing oil and pray for the Holy Spirit to visit you in your sleep. You will experience a heightened level of dreams, visions and visitations from the Spirit of God.

My Thoughts